Property of
◊ **Follett**
Training and Development Department

W9-ACV-073

Making Change Work for You:
How to Handle Organizational Change

Richard S. Deems, Ph.D.

Novations Training Solutions, Inc.
4621 121ST Street
Urbandale IA, 50323
1-888-776-8268
www.novationstraining.com

Making Change Work for You:
How to Handle Organizational Change

Richard S. Deems, Ph.D.
Copyright ©1995 by Richard S. Deems, Ph.D.

All rights reserved. No part of this publication may be reproduced, stored in a retrieval system, or transmitted, in any form or by any means, electronic, mechanical, photocopying, recording, or otherwise, without the prior written permission of the publisher.

This publication is designed to provide accurate and authoritative information in regard to the subject matter covered. It is sold with the understanding that neither the author nor the publisher is engaged in rendering legal, accounting, or other professional service. If legal advice or other expert assistance is required, the services of a competent professional should be sought.

Credits:
Novations Training Solutions, Inc.: Art Bauer
                                    Todd McDonald
                                    Leigh Lewis
Managing Editor: Karen Massetti Miller
Designer: Gayle O'Brien

Published by Novations Training Solutions, Inc.
4621 121ST Street
Urbandale IA, 50323

Library of Congress Catalog Card Number 95-75608
Deems, Richard S., Ph.D.
Making Change Work for You: How to Handle Organizational Change

Printed in the United States of America
1997
ISBN 1-884926-38-x

Introduction

If you're a person who is or soon will be going through some kind of organizational change—or someone who has gone through the change and now wants to make sense of it all—then this book is for you! This book will help you understand yourself and others and the dynamics of the change process. Its goal is to provide you with the information you need to become your own expert at making change work for you—whether it's organizational change or personal change.

Although we don't always welcome change, more times than not, it's actually a positive force in our lives. At least that's been my experience. As I look back at my personal and professional life, it's clear to me that, when there hasn't been enough change in my life, I went out and created it. As I tried to understand myself and my reactions to change, I read all I could find on the subject. Alvin Toffler's early book, *Future Shock,* got my total attention. So did a little volume called *Understanding Tomorrow* by a lesser known author, Lyle E. Schaller.

My doctoral research focused on what happens to people who go through the experience of moving from one community to another, and it taught me a great deal about change. Later, when I went through the experience of being fired from a job, I devoted a lot of personal energy analyzing my own reactions to the process of change. As my work evolved into helping others deal successfully with career change, I had even greater opportunity to focus on the process: I read, listened, remembered, analyzed, and formulated.

It seemed clear that, contrary to what I'd read in certain books, change is not a neat, linear, sequential kind of process that goes from endings to new beginnings. It's much more dynamic, more fluid, more interactive. If it were an amusement-park ride, it would be more like a roller coaster than a merry-go-round; if it were a shape, it would be more amoeboid than rectangular.

Since I first studied the change experience, I've worked with several thousand people who've experienced it firsthand. They've made invaluable contributions to this book by sharing their insights and providing feedback on the interactive exercises. You'll read about the success strategies many of them used to deal with change in their own lives.

Kathy Kolbe and her books, *The Conative Connection: Uncovering the Link Between Who You Are and How You Perform* (Addison Wesley, 1990) *and Pure Instinct: Business' Untapped Resource* (Times Books/Random House, 1993), have given me significant insight into how people differ in the ways they naturally respond to change. For example, Kolbe told me that I'm a person who has an instinct to thrive on change. She's right. But, as you'll discover in Chapter 4, not everyone has that same instinct.

There have been many people who, over the years, have contributed to this work, not the least of whom are the participants in my workshops and training sessions. Special thanks go to: consultant Dick Heiser, who helped me develop my first seminar on change, and the employees of the Federal Home Loan Bank, who were its first participants; the employees of Amoco Oil Company's Customer Service Center, who energetically added their insights on ways to deal with change; my graduate advisor, Dr. Roger Hiemstra, who helped me learn how adults learn; the cotrainers who have worked with me over the years; Todd McDonald for keeping me honest and logical in the way I presented this information; Leigh Lewis for managing the publishing process; Dave Kirchner for his editorial expertise; Art Bauer for his confidence in my work; my daughters, Terri A. Deems, soon-to-be Ph.D., for her patient sharing of her understandings about the change process, and Sonja Kay McKiness for her insights into the younger worker; and, finally, Sandie, the special person in my life who helped me put these insights on paper as only a special person can.

I hope you are able to use the information in this book to become your own expert at making change work for you!

How to Read This Book

This book has been designed to be as user-friendly as possible! The writing style is easy to understand, and the organization is easy to follow. Here are several suggestions to help you get the most from *Making Change Work for You:*

♦ First, take a few minutes to flip through the book, letting your eyes fall on whatever headings or paragraphs grab your attention and reading whatever interests you. Get acquainted with the book and how it's organized. Read the author's comments in the Introduction.

♦ Next, turn to the Table of Contents and look at the chapter titles and major topics. As you read the chapter titles, ask yourself, "What questions do I have about making change work for me?" Make a list of all of your questions.

♦ Then begin reading Chapter 1, "What's Going On in Your Life?" making sure to complete the interactive exercises. Your insights into what's really going on in your life will come into play in subsequent chapters, so it's important to write out your answers to the exercises.

♦ Continue reading the book. The next chapters will explore the situations that are bringing you here in the first place. They'll look into how much you already know about change and change in the workplace and how we naturally vary in our reactions to change. Later chapters will give you the strategies you need to make change work for you, including tips on managing the stress that often accompanies change. The last chapter will help you systematically implement the strategies that can make change work for you!

After you've read the book from cover to cover and completed the interactive exercises and Chapter Reviews, you may want to return to the sections you found most helpful to reinforce the points they make. Here are some tips to help you:

♦ Take a sheet of paper and write out three questions you still have about organizational change. In your first question, identify a key word or phrase that might indicate where in the book you'll find the answer.
♦ Return to the Table of Contents and skim the chapter titles and major topics to identify the areas where you might find the answer. Reread the material in those sections until your question has been answered.

◆ Repeat this procedure for the rest of your questions. As you find answers to each of them, you may come up with still others. If you do, just continue the process.

The publisher and author hope you find this book insightful and helpful, and that it will be one you frequently pull off the shelf to revisit. Our goal is to help you become your own expert at making change work for you!

About the Author

Richard S. Deems, Ph.D., has more than 20 years experience working with individuals and companies going through change. He has personally experienced termination, reorganizations, and career change. The systems he has developed make the change process easier and more effective for both organizations and employees. In *Making Change Work for You,* Deems presents his time-tested strategies so people know how to view change as opportunity.

"When employees know how to make change work for themselves," Deems asserts, "they also know how to make it work for the organization."

A popular workshop leader, Deems has conducted training programs from coast to coast and in Canada. He is equally comfortable working with senior executives as well as entry-evel employees. Deems is also author of *Interviewing: More Than a Gut Feeling* and *I Have to Fire Someone!* from Novations Training Solutions, Inc.

Deems received his bachelor's degree from Nebraska Wesleyan University, his master's degree from Northwestern University, and his doctorate from the University of Nebraska at Lincoln with an emphasis in adult learning and development.

● Table of Contents

Chapter Five

Managing the Stress That Comes with Change 60

Chapter Six

How Work Teams React to Organizational Change 76

Chapter Seven

How Work Teams Can Survive Downsizing 92

Chapter Eight

Your Action Plan for Making Change Work 102

Chapter *One*

What's Going On in Your Life?

Chapter Objectives

▶ Review your situation regarding change.

▶ Describe the change that is taking place or that has already taken place.

▶ Identify the questions you have about how to make change work for you.

Something is going on in your life that involves change. Otherwise, you wouldn't have picked up this book. You may be going through a change at your workplace. Or perhaps the organization where you work just went through some major change—or is preparing to. Whatever your situation, this book can be a special resource for you.

As you read this book, you will learn a number of things. You'll find out:

◆ Why some people respond to change one way, while others react differently.

◆ How change always has been—and will continue to be—a part of your life.

◆ How to manage the stress that might come as a result of organizational change.

◆ The usual way work teams react to organizational change.

◆ Things you can do to make surviving a downsizing easier.

◆ How to put this information into action to make change work for you.

Your Situation

What's going on in your life that brings you to this book? Is your employer going through an organizational change right now? Or has your company just gone through the change? Does your company plan to implement a change in the next several weeks or months? What kind of change?

Take a Moment

Take time to summarize your situation and the organizational change you're experiencing (or have undergone or are anticipating.) Your summary can be brief, like the following example:

■ The company where I've worked for the past seven years is going through a reorganization. They have had a reengineering team working for the past year, and the announcements will be made next month. There are lots of rumors, and I'm worried about my job.

Your summary doesn't need to be long, but it does need to state what is taking place.

Here is a brief description of the organizational change I'm going through or will be going through:

_____

_____

_____

_____

Though this book deals primarily with making organizational change work for you, organizational change often has an impact on people's personal lives, too. You may be going through personal changes as a result of the organizational changes. Is the company change affecting your personal life? Is it having an impact on your family? on your relationships? on your energy level? on your economic situation? Are you going through personal changes, too?

Take a Moment

In the space below, briefly describe any personal changes you may be going through as a result of the present, past, or anticipated organizational changes where you work. Here's an example:

■ The kids are in high school now, and one will be in college next year. If my job gets eliminated or I have to take a pay cut, our plans will have to change. Things are getting stressful at home as we all worry about what the announcements will bring.

Here is a brief description of how the company change is affecting my personal life—my relationships, my family, my career, and my finances:

_____

_____

_____

_____

Now that you've reviewed and described the situation that brings you to this book, it will be easier to review your personal history and identify how you typically deal with change. How you dealt with change in the past is important information because it will help you capitalize on areas of strength and note areas that need more attention as you learn to make change work for you.

By the time we reach adulthood, we've already developed a good number of skills for dealing with change.

Your History

By the time we reach adulthood, we've already developed a good number of skills for dealing with change. After all, we've had to deal with the changes of growing from an infant to a child, to a teenager, and finally to an adult. In the course of those changes, we developed a set of skills—our own personal history—for dealing with change.

By reviewing your history and identifying how you tend to react to change, you can evaluate your skills to make sure you're doing all you can to make change work for you. To review your history, start by thinking about previous organizational changes you've experienced and how you handled them. Maybe the change involved dealing with a new boss, new coworkers, a new assignment, or new technology. Here's an example:

■ This is an organizational change I experienced:
   • Got transferred to a new office.

■ And this is how I reacted:
   • Hard to say good-bye to my friends, but made new friends quickly.

Take a Moment

Use the space below to summarize how you reacted to at least three previous experiences of dealing with organizational change.

Think of three times you experienced some form of organizational change. Briefly describe each change and how you reacted to it:

This is an organizational change I experienced:

1. _____

2. _____

3. _____

And this is how I reacted:

1. _____

2. _____

3. _____

Organizational change often has at least some impact on our personal lives, too. Just as we've developed a history of how we've reacted to organizational change, we also have a history of how we've dealt with personal change.

Take a Moment

In the space below, summarize three instances of personal change you've experienced. Try to identify instances in which the personal change was a direct result of an organizational change. Just as before, briefly describe each event and explain how you responded to the change experiences.

Think of three times you experienced some form of personal change. Briefly describe each event and how you reacted to it:

This is a personal change I experienced:

1. _____

2. _____

3. _____

And this is how I reacted:

1. _____

2. _____

3. _____

As you completed these exercises, did you gain some new insights into how you tend to react to change? Do you see a pattern or trend in the ways you've dealt with change in the past? Or did you find several patterns? Perhaps you found no pattern at all.

Take a Moment

Take time to reread your responses to the two previous exercises. Then write a brief summary of your personal history of reacting to change. One way to approach this exercise is to start with the words, "I learned that . . ." and complete the sentence. Your descriptions don't need to be lengthy, but they do need to include enough information to let you use them later. Here are two examples:

■ Example 1: I learned that I vary in the ways I react to change. Often I deal with change in the workplace easier than change in my personal life. New assignments are a challenge, but having to work with a new boss sometimes upsets me. In my personal life, I learned that relationships and friends are important. When a friend moves away, it takes me time to adjust.

■ Example 2: I learned that I usually deal with change pretty well. I thought I didn't, but as I look at my history, I realize I take things in stride, ask a lot of questions, and then make up my own mind about things. I tend to try to separate changes in the workplace from my personal life.

With these two examples in mind, take the time to write your own description of how you usually respond to change.

After thinking about my history and ways I've dealt with organizational change and personal change in the past, I learned that:

_____

_____

_____

_____

As you describe your situation and your history, you'll probably come up with even more questions than you had before you started reading this chapter. Here's your chance to get them out in the open!

Your Questions

What are your questions? Do you wonder if you react to change the way other people do? Do you wonder why some people respond to change in one way, while others respond to the same change differently? Do you wonder if you really can make change work for you?

Before you can make change work for you, you need to be honest and realistic about your questions and any fears or concerns you may have.

Before you can make change work for you, you need to be honest and realistic about your questions and any fears or concerns you may have. You'll find it helpful to read the questions that follow and check any that are the same or similar to those you have. Here they are—examples of questions others have asked:

◆ What will happen to me?

◆ Will I still have a job?

◆ Will I work with the same people?

◆ Why do I fear the unknown?

◆ Why do people seem to react to change in different ways?

◆ Is there one way of reacting to change that's better than another?

◆ What happens to work teams that go through organizational change?

◆ Will there be even more changes in the workplace?

◆ Why do I resist change?

◆ Why do I go looking for change?

◆ Will my past contributions be taken into consideration?

◆ How can I manage the stress I'm feeling because of this organizational change?

◆ How will my pay and benefits be figured?

◆ Will I have to learn new skills?

◆ Am I too young? too old? too much in the middle?

◆ Is change always negative?

- Is change always positive?

- Will this book really help me learn to make change work for me?

1

Take a Moment

What other questions do you have about making change work for you? Are your questions similar or different from those of other people who work with you? What questions do your coworkers ask? What are your five biggest questions? Before reading further, finish writing out your responses to this exercise.

List the top five questions you have about organizational change, how you react to change, and how you can make change work for you:

1. _____

2. _____

3. _____

4. _____

5. _____

Congratulations! In reading this first chapter and completing its interactive exercises, either by yourself or as part of a group training session, you've done some serious thinking. After all, you've been asked to put down on paper some of your innermost thoughts about organizational change and how it's affecting your personal life.

You may have found reading this chapter exhilarating, exhausting, or maybe even troubling. But your efforts will be rewarded. In the chapters that follow, you'll refer often to these early exercises and the personal insights you wrote about. So if for any reason you haven't completed all of the exercises, please go back and finish them now.

By completing each exercise, you'll be helping yourself learn how to make change work for you!

Chapter *Two*

What We Know About Change

Chapter Objectives

▶ Understand why self-chosen change is the easiest kind of change.

▶ Recognize that we are what we are because of change.

▶ See how the way work gets done is changing.

▶ Understand why change affecting relationships often is the most difficult change.

▶ Recognize that change is constant.

Change is everywhere around us, and we deal with it all the time.

Change is everywhere around us, and we deal with it all the time. The changing of the seasons. Changes in the weather. Even a change of clothes. But although we may experience change all the time, we seldom stop to really analyze what we know about it.

In order to develop and implement your own personal strategy for making change work for you, you need to understand several basic concepts about change. Here are five concepts that can help you understand the role of change in your life.

Self-Chosen Change Is the Easiest

Change that we choose ourselves is the easiest kind to experience. This is true whether it happens to be organizational change or personal change. When we make the conscious decision to go through some kind of change, we usually understand that it may involve some discomfort. But in making the decision, we also decide to make the best of any stress or unpleasantness the change may bring. It's our choice. We probably weighed the pluses and minuses, and decided to go ahead with the change anyway.

Change that's not of our own choosing, however, is more difficult to deal with. Change that's imposed on us often is change we resist; we may see only the minuses and few of the pluses. Unfortunately, organizational change usually is change over which we have little, if any, control. We're out of the decision-making loop. Others make the decisions that affect us.

We learn early, however, that if we want to continue working for the organization, we must make adjustments. But our decision about how to react to organizational change really is our own. After all, we can decide it's unfair, or we can decide it's inconvenient, or we even can decide that the change is positive! What's important to know is that *we can learn to make change work for us, even when it's imposed on us and not of our own choice.*

2

> **Change that's imposed on us often is change we resist.**

Take a Moment

Is the change you have experienced, are experiencing, or will be going through, change that is imposed? Or do you really have a choice in whether or not to experience it? Briefly summarize your situation and how much the change is imposed and how much choice you think you have.

_____

_____

_____

_____

We Are What We Are Because of Change

Change has been a part of life since birth. It's that way for all of us. We simply are what we are because we've gone through all kinds of change. We learned how to tie our shoes, how to dress ourselves, how to read, how to do math. We learned how to ride a bicycle, how to avoid getting called on in class when we were unprepared, how to deal with bullies, how to survive finding out that the special person in our life doesn't know we exist, and on and on and on.

We are what we are because we've experienced—and survived—a great deal of change. And that change has had various effects on our lives. For example, here are some ways that change affects us:

- ◆ We learned the skills we needed to do a job, and then we went out and got a job. The result? We can pay for food, housing, clothes, and so on.

- ◆ We may have had a pet die, or a close friend die, or maybe even a parent. The result? We know the feelings of disappointment and loss, and those experiences have changed the way we think of relationships.

- ◆ We went out, exercised, and worked up a sweat. The result? We learned that we looked and felt better when we exercise, and that it's a great way to relieve stress.

Enough? Okay, you get the idea.

We are what we are because of the changes we've already experienced. Those changes aren't always likable or enjoyable. Sometimes they're tragic. But they've shaped us and our actions and reactions, and they've made us what we are.

We are what we are because of the changes we've already experienced.

Here is one person's review of recent life changes and the effects of those changes:

Change	How it has affected me
New job at ABC Company	Really enjoy going to work!
Melissa began school	Time is more important and more difficult to find.
Spouse got caught in downsizing	Not easy. Takes a lot of extra energy and time to help spouse deal with the job loss.
Will have new supervisor next month	Means more responsibility — I'm ready for it!

We may not always like the changes that come our way, but we are what we are because of them.

Take a Moment

With these examples in mind, use the space below to complete your own listing of a couple major changes you've experienced in the past two years, and the impact each has had on you.

Change	How it has affected me
_____	_____
	_____
_____	_____
	_____
_____	_____
	_____

The Way Work Gets Done Is Rapidly Changing

There have been many changes in the workplace in the past 20 years, and there will be many more in the years ahead. Many of these changes have been the result of new technology, but others have occurred because of societal changes, global economic changes, and changes in the ways organizations are structured.

New Technology

New technology has created new fields, such as telemarketing, while at the same time drastically changing the way work gets done. Here are just three examples:

> New technology has created new fields, such as telemarketing, while at the same time drastically changing the way work gets done.

◆ In many companies, managers have PCs on their desks instead of access to a secretarial pool. They are expected to learn the appropriate software and to use their computers for certain secretarial functions.

◆ As computers have become more powerful, entire job fields have been eliminated. The field of publishing has seen some of the most dramatic changes. Gone now are the typesetters and the graphic designers who did their work by hand. Now it's all done by just a few people at computers.

◆ Faster, more powerful computers are having an impact on other fields, too. For example, a good deal of the insurance-underwriting function now is being handled by computer, reducing the need for underwriters. Changing technology brings a changing workplace.

Changing Population

The population of the United State is aging, and the average age of workers will continue to increase. The percentage of workers under age 30 is expected to decline in the next 20 years, and so will the number of workers available for entry-level jobs. The full impact of these changes isn't clear, but they're certain to change the way work gets done.

Competition

The need for U.S. companies to remain competitive with their foreign counterparts also is having an impact on the way work gets done. The need to compete has resulted in mergers, acquisitions, consolidations, and of course, layoffs.

The push seems to be for the highest quality product at the absolute lowest cost, regardless of source. As large investors demand higher returns on their investments, they are increasingly less concerned about where their returns come from. Corporate purchasing personnel know this and look for ways to continually cut costs. If a foreign supplier can produce a similar or better product at lower cost, it likely will be favored with the purchasing contract.

The bottom line: Cost of goods matters more than their country of origin. Cost-cutting will continue to be a hot topic and definitely will continue to affect the way work gets done.

Organizational Structure

Companies have been flattening their organizational structures for some time. Now they have fewer mid-level managers, which means there is less opportunity for advancement: more and more people will have to accept lateral moves instead of making a continual climb up the corporate ladder. Some people even are saying that the goal of climbing the corporate ladder has become unrealistic and out-of-date.

More and more people will have to accept lateral moves instead of making a continual climb up the corporate ladder.

Increasingly, instead of having a "career," a worker essentially contracts with a company to perform a set of tasks. Once those tasks—and the worker's assignment—are completed, the worker negotiates another contract with perhaps a different company for a new set of tasks. What will the eventual impact be? We can't know for sure, but what we do know is that the way work gets done is changing!

These are just some examples of how the way work gets done is changing. We can't know for certain what the workplace will look like in the year 2001. But what we do know is that the workplace of today will continue to change.

Take a Moment

Think about some of the changes in your workplace in the past few years and the changes that are being talked about for the future. Make your own list of how the way work is getting done is changing within your field or your company:

1. _____

2. _____

3. _____

4. _____

5. _____

As the workplace changes, so must the people who inhabit it. Change that affects work relationships, however, often is the most difficult kind to experience.

Change That Affects Relationships Is More Difficult

Although technological or organizational change often takes place rapidly, change that involves interpersonal relationships tends to take longer. A department can be reorganized—even downsized—in a very short time. A year later, however, the people in that department still may talk about the changes they went through and how those changes affected them.

Even when it may seem all right to change how we do our work, we still may resist changes that affect whom we work with. The more people like working together, the more difficult it is for them to go through a personnel change.

Even when it may seem all right to change how we do our work, we still may resist changes that affect whom we work with.

This may explain, in part, why productivity typically increases when a company makes an announcement that it's closing a facility or eliminating a work group or team. If the employees have an especially good working relationship, they tend to increase their productivity. As one person explained, "We worked harder, hoping that if the decision-makers saw how productive we were, they wouldn't go through with the changes. Then we all could continue working together."

2

The dynamic seems to go like this:

If you don't enjoy the people you work with, you're ready for any kind of change that will put you in contact with coworkers you may like better. You welcome change, applaud it, anticipate it. But if you already like the people you work with, it's not as easy to go through organizational change. It takes longer to adjust, to regain confidence in the company, and to trust your new coworkers.

If you perform your job primarily by yourself, having to change the way you work may be little more than an inconvenience. You may have to learn new procedures or tasks, but the overall impact of the change is minimal.

But if your work depends on others and the quality of those working relationships is high, any organizational change will have a much greater impact. It will take more time and energy for you to adjust. After all, you'll have to develop new relationships, and you probably wonder how long it will take to trust these new people.

When an employee leaves a group of coworkers who enjoyed working with him or her, the remaining employees experience a sense of personal loss. A grieving process sets in. It takes longer for them to adjust to the change than if the work unit had been left intact.

> **When an employee leaves a group of coworkers who enjoyed working with him or her, the remaining employees experience a sense of personal loss.**

Take a Moment

Review your first list of changes that you've experienced in the past two years (page 21). Indicate below those changes that involved relationships. For each item, ask yourself, "Was this change more difficult or easier for me to deal with?"

1. _____

2. _____

3. _____

4. _____

5. _____

Change Is Constant

About a year ago, I interviewed 50 managers and executives from across the country who represented the banking, manufacturing, services, insurance, communications, and retail fields. When I asked them, "What are the emerging issues your company will have to deal with in the next five years?" almost all of them replied, "Change!" As one executive put it, "Change is constant. And the pace of change will accelerate rather than decrease."

In the next 10 years, there will be more—not less—change in the workplace.

Like it or not, change is with us. It's here to stay. One thing you can count on in the next 10 years is that you will continue to experience organizational change. There will be more, not less, change occurring in the workplace. You can fight it, or you can learn how to make it work for you. It's your choice.

Self-Check: Chapter 2 Review

Complete the following sentences.

1. Change that is _____ is the easiest change to go through.

2. We are what we are because of _____.

2

3. The way _____ is getting done is rapidly changing.

4. The most difficult change is change that deals with

   _____.

5. Change is _____.

Chapter*Three*

Strategies for Making Change Work

Chapter Objective

▶ Master 10 strategies to help make change work for you.

You've taken time to think about the situation that brings you to this book, and you've considered several basic concepts about change. In this chapter, you'll learn 10 strategies that can help make change work for you!

These 10 strategies come directly from the experiences of thousands of people who themselves have gone through change. Those people struggled with organizational change and its impact on their personal lives and survived.

They did not allow change to get to them, but instead turned what could have been negative experiences into positive experiences. They made change work for them.

As you read about each strategy, ask yourself:

◆ **Am I willing to do something instead of nothing?**
   Without the commitment to make change work for you, these strategies will have little opportunity to make a difference. You make the difference when you commit to do something instead of nothing.

◆ **Am I willing to take a calculated risk?**
   Yes, there's risk involved in using any of these strategies. There's always risk when you deal with change; it's part of what change is all about. We can never be 100 percent

certain of what change will bring. But without taking risk, people would never move away from home, find a job, make a friend, fall in love, and all kinds of other nice things. Remember, there's also a risk in doing nothing.

◆ **When can I put this strategy into action?**
Some of these strategies involve mind-set—how a person thinks about change. Other strategies involve specific actions for you to take. Reading this chapter won't be enough. You must commit to putting as many of these strategies into action as you can.

Strategy 1: Anticipate Workplace Change and Be Ready for It

3

Change is with us, and it's here to stay. The changes organizations are experiencing now will continue, and the speed with which more changes occur probably will increase by the end of this century. We can choose now to be ready for it!

The first strategy to make change work for you is to accept that the workplace will continue to change. Once you know about and accept change, you can anticipate it, prepare for it, and decide to make it work for you!

How can you prepare for accelerated workplace change? Reading this book is one way. Completing the interactive exercises in each chapter is another. Putting the strategies into action is perhaps the most important way of all.

The key is that you honestly accept workplace change as a fact of life. Instead of resisting it or even actively fighting it, consciously decide to make it work for you. It's a mind-set strategy—and a very important one! When you anticipate workplace change and realize that it will continue to take place, you can prepare for it.

> The first strategy to make change work for you is to accept that the workplace will continue to change.

Take a Moment

What are some of the changes you think will take place in your workplace in the next six months? in the next year? What can you do to prepare yourself for each change?

_____

_____

_____

_____

Strategy 2: View Change as Opportunity

With every change in our lives, there have been new opportunities.

Several years ago, while leading a workshop on career change, a participant came up and said something like this: "Dick, whenever I think of change, I think CEO."

"That's nice," I responded, waiting for the person to continue.

"Sure," she said, "CEO—Change Equals Opportunity! If you want to be CEO of your life, you need to think like a CEO. And CEO can mean Change Equals Opportunity!"

She was very insightful. This second strategy asks you to think of change as opportunity. Without change, neither you nor I would be where we are today. Change has broadened our horizons, has enabled us to grow, and has brought us to today. With every change in our lives, there have been new opportunities.

The same things can happen in the workplace.

When people believe change is negative, they don't find much exciting about it. But if people believe CEO, Change Equals Opportunity, they are ready for change and will look for the new opportunities that are inherent with it!

> # Take a Moment
>
> Think about some of the changes you've experienced in the past year in your workplace. For each change, list as many of the positive opportunities as you can think of that occurred as a result of the change:
>
> _____
>
> _____
>
> _____
>
> _____

3

Strategy 3: Practice Effective Stress-Management Strategies

If you're feeling stressed, as some people do when their companies go through organizational change, you should practice stress-management strategies. Good stress management means:

- Control your emotions instead of letting your emotions control you.

- Don't pay much attention to rumors.

- Accept that change takes place at all companies.

- Take care of yourself physically.

- Keep from acting out of anger.

Chapter 5, "Managing the Stress That Comes with Change," presents strategies to deal with the stress that comes from organizational change.

Control your emotions instead of letting your emotions control you.

Strategy 4: Ask the Consultant's Question

Consultants are a part of today's workplace. They can help in a variety of ways, and many are on the cutting edge of identifying new efficiencies. How do they do it? Many consultants approach their work with one major question in mind: *What needs doing that isn't getting done or that could be done better?*

As you perform your own job, look for things that need to be done and aren't being done, or things you think could be done better. As you identify those items, take it a step further and try to identify possible solutions.

Here are some specific examples others have come up with—simply because they took the time to ask the consultant's question:

Companies seek out employees who look for ways to do things better, more efficiently, or with fewer resources.

■ If the recycling scrap bin were moved just 10 feet, it would take less time to dispose of scrap and, because of having more scrap to recycle, cut our costs. How did this happen? Someone realized that a lot of scrap was just being tossed on the floor and discarded. The reason it wasn't being thrown into the recycling bin was that the bin was too far away. By moving the scrap bin 10 feet closer to the work station, employees would use it—and reduce costs!

■ A computer program can be designed to eliminate redundant paperwork so that when an order is entered, it automatically sets up the billing form, addresses the shipping label, and enters the order-processing information into the appropriate schedule. Why? Because someone realized that with the power of computers, there had to be a way to enter information once and make it do more than just one thing.

■ In most households today, both husband and wife work. They don't like to take extra time to do their banking, such as making a consumer loan or even talking with someone about a home mortgage. But if the bank were located where they go at least once each week—the grocery store—it would be different. And now it's common to find full-service bank offices in supermarkets.

What needs doing that isn't being done—or that could be done better—in your organization?

When you have an idea that you believe will save time, money, or just make the work more pleasant—tell someone. Who? Maybe your boss is the person to talk with. Maybe your boss's boss is the right person. Maybe it's your other team members who need to know.

Be prepared to talk about the problem and how your solution will help. Who knows? Maybe you'll be the right person to head the team or unit that solves the problem.

Companies seek out employees who look for ways to do things better, more efficiently, or with fewer resources. Just ask the consultant's question and make change work for you!

What needs doing that isn't being done—or that could be done better— in your organization?

3

Take a Moment

1. What are some of the changes in your company that have resulted from the suggestions of employees?

   _____

   _____

   _____

   _____

2. Set aside one day this week to ask the consultant's question while you do your work. Keep a pad of paper handy to jot down your findings. For each item you identify, see if you can describe a solution.

Strategy 5: Get Your Work Done Accurately and On Time

One of the consequences of organizational change is that some people stop doing their work. They've responded to organizational change by giving up, by doing nothing. Maybe they will regain their sense of productivity and maybe not. What those employees do, however, should have no bearing on what you decide to do.

> **Even if you don't like the organizational change, you can make a difference.**

What's important for you, regardless of your long-range plans, is that you do your work accurately and on time. Even if you don't like the organizational change, you can make a difference. After all, it's in your best interest to do your work accurately and on time. Here are two reasons:

First, management watches and observes and remembers. When there's a future promotion opportunity or someone is needed for a special project, management will look to those who helped during the change—even if they didn't particularly like what took place. If you're one of those who continues to do good work, it will be noticed and remembered. In other words, it's in your self-interest to continue to do your work satisfactorily.

Second, when you took your job, you and the company made an agreement. You agreed to trade your time, your knowledge, your energy, your brainpower, or your muscle to get something done; in return, you get a paycheck. It doesn't make any difference what that something is; it can be making widgets, approving loans, entering data, or crafting custom windows. The agreement is that you trade your time and energy to get something done in return for a paycheck.

Even in the midst of organizational change, it's important to keep your part of the bargain. There will be others who don't. But unless they hinder you in getting your work done, those people aren't your worry. Your concern is to be true to yourself and to do things that, over the long haul, will help.

It's in your best interest to get your work done accurately and on time, even when you don't feel like it. When you do, you'll be making change work for you!

Take a Moment

Ask yourself three questions:

1. "Have I been getting things done on time, even if I don't agree with the organizational change?" If so, then congratulate yourself. If not, ask yourself, "Is not getting things done really in my best interest?"

2. "Are there ways I can be even more helpful during this time of change?" If so, list several ways you can be more helpful, and mark those that you can do or complete this week or this month.

3. "Are my attitude and actions consistent with doing things that are in my best interest?" If so, tell others. If not, ask what you will get in return for not getting things done on time and up to standards.

3

Strategy 6: Build Bridges: Give the New People a Chance

New people are a part of most organizational change. Maybe your company has a new president or a new vice president. Maybe you have a new manager. Maybe you find yourself working with new people in a new work unit or team. Give the new people a chance.

They probably have reservations, too. It's natural. Remember what we know about change—that if we liked the people we worked with before, we tend to set up barriers to the new people. Build bridges, not fences. Give the new people a chance.

For example:

■ Let's suppose you find yourself part of a new work unit. There are nine of you: seven have worked together before and two of you are new. What are you going to do to try to fit in?

   1. Take time to get acquainted. Find extra time (at lunches, breaks, breakfasts, or after hours) to get to know the original people. What have they been doing? Do they enjoy it? What do they think are the problems this new unit

will experience? Find out as much as you can about these new people because, in the process, you'll probably find you like working with them, just as you enjoyed working with your last group.

2. Learn the agenda. Find out the priorities of this new unit. Find out how the unit prefers to work. Let them know the conditions under which you're most productive, and find out how they are most productive.

3. Get interested in these new people. After all, you'll be spending about a third of each day working with them. You'll all enjoy it more if you have an interest in what these people do and what their lives are like. You'll also be more productive, which leads to even greater job satisfaction.

The more we know about people, the easier it is to like them. Give the new people a chance!

Take a Moment

List at least three things you can do to give new people a chance:

1. _____

2. _____

3. _____

Strategy 7: Look for Ways to Do More

Be ready and willing to take on a new assignment; it will be noticed.

There are always lots of things that don't seem to get done during any organizational change. Instead of wasting energy trying to assign blame or worrying about why those things aren't getting done, step up and do more yourself!

Be ready and willing to take on a new assignment, to stay late so that an important project gets done on time, or to take on extra responsibility. It will be noticed. Those who are managing the change will see that you're willing to step in and do more when it's needed. They'll see that you're not blocking change but are helping things to work more smoothly.

In other words, you become the kind of employee the company wants and needs. This is the kind of employee who usually gets pegged for promotion, who emerges as a leader, or who receives special recognition for getting things done.

You'll notice that you're being noticed. You'll also notice that, because you're willing to invest more time and energy in your work, you're probably enjoying your job more, too.

3

Take a Moment

Take some time to assess what's going on in your work area. Are there things that aren't getting done that need to get done? List them in the space below. Identify those tasks that you could help get completed.

_____

_____

_____

_____

Strategy 8: Exit If You Must

Sometimes an organizational change is such that you realize you just can't adjust to it. The stress is too great, or you fundamentally disagree with it, or there's some other compelling reason.

It doesn't do you or the company any good to continue working at a place where you don't want to be. You won't be productive, and you won't have job satisfaction. Those who work with you certainly won't enjoy it. Even your health may suffer.

The best strategy? Exit.

If there is a voluntary severance plan, volunteer for it. If not, identify what you want your next job to be. Also identify the kind of work environment in which you can be productive and satisfied at the same time. Develop your job-search strategy, and make the move as quickly as possible.

> It doesn't do you or the company any good to continue working at a place where you don't want to be.

Remember, however, that until you exit, you still need to satisfactorily do your work. You may not always feel like it, but it's important that you do. If you don't, it's likely that the word will get around, and successfully exiting and joining a new company could become much more difficult.

Strategy 9: Tell Others About the Results of Your Work

The best way to help managers place you where you can be the most successful is to tell others about the results of your work.

As the pace of change increases, companies will look to their employees to help managers place people where they can be the most successful. The best way to help managers place you where you can be the most successful is to tell others about the results of your work. Here's how to do it.

1. Make a list of the things you do in your job. List the special projects you're involved in, the special teams you're part of, or any special assignments you've taken on. Make your list as detailed as possible.

2. For each of the items on your list, ask yourself, "So what?" You want to identify the results of your work, and asking yourself, "So what?" is the single most helpful way to get at those results. Here are two examples:

■ Let's say you process statements at a credit center. You list the things you do and begin to ask, "So what?" As you ponder the results of your work, you begin to realize that you have a number of them, which might include:
  * Reduced error rate to less than 1 percent.
  * Commended by customers for being courteous and prompt with information.
  * Designed new input form that reduced data-entry time by more than 30 percent.
  * Trained new employee in data entry, and assisted him in reducing error rate from 6 percent to less than 2 percent within two weeks.
  * Served on the team that evaluates procedures and recommended ways to streamline processing.

■ Let's say you're a supervisor for a shipping department. As you analyze all that you do, you begin to realize that you've had some great results, which might include:

- Team processed all orders within 24 hours and with error rate of less than 1 in 100.
- Led team in process-improvement program, and identified 11 ways to reduce costs.
- Reorganized shipping line, which reduced packaging costs by more than 20 percent.
- Assisted delivery drivers in revising loading procedures to reduce time on the route.
- Researched and identified new packaging materials that reduced postage by 35 percent.

Why focus on results? Because the results you've achieved are a strong indicator of what you do best. What you do best typically is what you most enjoy doing. And what you most enjoy doing typically are the kinds of things in which you're the most successful!

3

3. After you identify the results of your work, you need to tell others. You can:

◆ Mention your results to your supervisor during staff meetings or informal meetings:

■ Todd, I did an analysis on the time it takes us to get an order in the mail, and I thought you'd like to know that we've reduced packaging time by more than 30 percent.

◆ Make sure that your written reports include statements about the results of your work:

■ The process-improvement team designed a new order-fulfillment process that reduced packaging time by more than 30 percent.

◆ Make a small poster, and place it where others in your unit can see it:

■ In December, our work unit reduced errors to below the goal of 2 percent!

◆ You'll think of still other ways to let people know about the results of your work.

Take a Moment

1. Make a list of at least 10 things you do on your job, or 10 things you've been involved in at work in the past year, such as special teams or committees. For each item, ask yourself, "So what? What happened because I did . . . ?" Write a statement for each item on your list to describe the results of your work.

1. _____

2. _____

3. _____

4. _____

5. _____

6. _____

7. _____

8. _____

9. _____

10. _____

2. List at least three different ways you can tell others about the results of your work.

1. _____

2. _____

3. _____

Strategy 10: Be Someone Others Enjoy Working With

Nobody likes to work alongside a grouch, a complainer, or a negative person. Instead of being a grouch or a complainer, be someone others enjoy working with. Be someone who has a positive attitude, who smiles, who says "please" and "thank you."

> **No one likes to work alongside a negative person.**

Be someone others like to talk with, to work alongside, to eat lunch with. Be someone who's enjoyable to work with. Smile. Laugh. Compliment others. Get things done. Lend a helping hand when it's needed. Show interest in others. Build people up. Help out.

When you're a person others enjoy working with:

◆ More gets done.

◆ Work is less stressful.

◆ It's more satisfying to go to work.

◆ The whole workplace is more enjoyable.

◆ You know how to make change work for you!

There always will be those who grumble in the midst of change, who see only the drawbacks and not the opportunities. Let them be that way, if they insist. But for you, however, it's more important to be someone others enjoy working with. It's not only more fun, but it's the key to making change work for you!

3

Self-Check: Chapter 3 Review

1. Review each of the strategies. Identify at least three that you can implement this week.

   1. _____

      _____

   2. _____

      _____

   3. _____

      _____

2. Make a list of those characteristics that you believe make someone else enjoyable to work with. After you've made your list, review it again and put a check mark next to those items that describe you as well.

   _____

   _____

   _____

   _____

Chapter *Four*

Why People React Differently to Change

Chapter Objectives

▶ Explain why people react to change differently.

▶ Recognize four conative action modes and their relationship to change.

▶ Identify how people can use their natural strengths during organizational change.

By now, you've noticed that not everybody reacts to organiza-tional change the way you do! You already knew that, but being reminded of it won't hurt. How did you come to know that? By watching others. As you observed coworkers and friends reacting to change, you realized they did so in different ways. You realized that not everyone reacts to change the way you do.

If you kept track of your observations, you may have noticed that during an organizational change, some of your coworkers wanted to know more about the change and why it was necessary, others wanted to know the details of how things were going to be reorganized, and still others seemed energized by the prospect of the change.

As you listened to individuals react to organizational change, you probably kept hearing words and phrases such as:

◆ "Why?"

◆ "Yeah, but . . ."

◆ "Why not?"

◆ "Well, show me!"

You probably also noticed that some even seemed to ask "Why?" one day and "Why not?" the next.

The system that answers the most questions and provides the most sensible information about how individuals react to change is based on the concept of *conation*. This chapter will introduce you to conation, explain why people react to change in different ways, and describe the four major ways people naturally react to change.

4

This chapter will introduce you to a paradigm that provides a reasonable, practical, and simple approach to actions and the natural ways people get things done. It will help you understand the various actions and reactions of your coworkers as they go through organizational change. After all, actions speak louder than words.

Conation—How We Naturally Get Things Done

Ancient philosophers talked about three parts of the mind: the parts that govern thinking, feeling, and doing. The thinking part is referred to as *intelligence*, or the *cognitive* part of the mind. The feeling part is referred to as *personality*, or the *affective* part of the mind. And the doing part is referred to as *instinct*, or the *conative* part of the mind.

The conative part of the mind has to do with:

◆ How we naturally and instinctively get things done.

◆ Actions, not feelings.

◆ The natural instincts each person has for striving to accomplish things.

> The conative part of the mind has to do with how we naturally and instinctively get things done.

45

The concept of conation was rediscovered in our country by management specialist Kathy Kolbe. After spending several years researching the subject, Kolbe developed a system to help people understand their natural conative talents.

The Kolbe Conative Action Modes™

Kolbe's research indicated that there are four separate action modes out of which people naturally and instinctively get things done—like reacting to organizational change. Kolbe calls these four action modes *Fact Finder, Follow Thru, Quick Start,* and *Implementor.* Her research also indicated that each person has natural talents in all four action modes, but usually more energy in one or two modes and less in the others.

Kolbe also asserts that no action mode is better than any other. It's not better to be a Fact Finder or a Quick Start than it is to be a Follow Thru or an Implementor. Each action mode makes contributions to every organization, and all action modes are needed for total effectiveness.

Kolbe's research found that our individual conative talent isn't a matter of heredity or environment. Instead, it's like a thumbprint—it just is! And, it doesn't change over time. A person's conative makeup is basically the same at age 55 as it was at age 5. It may be more understood and appreciated at 55, but it was there all along. Kolbe's research also found that there are no conative instincts that are just for men or just for women.

When we use our natural talents and have the freedom to do things the way we instinctively do them, we're energized and fully productive, and we enjoy what we're doing. When we have to work "against the grain"—not the way we'd naturally do things—we become stressed.

> **When we use our natural talents and have the freedom to do things the way we instinctively do them, we're energized and fully productive, and we enjoy what we're doing.**

To help you understand the various ways people respond to change, here are descriptions of the four action modes identified by Kolbe. Although only the Kolbe A Index™ (see page 58 for more information) can specifically identify your conative makeup, you can gain an appreciation of your conative instincts by reviewing these descriptions. As you read the description for each action mode, think about:

◆ Yourself and how you naturally get things done.

◆ Others with whom you work, and how you've observed them get things done.

You'll find it helpful to circle or highlight those words that seem to describe your own most natural actions.

Fact Finder

Fact Finder is the action mode out of which a person naturally and instinctively probes and gathers information. It is out of this action mode that a person is:

◆ Practical	◆ Objective	◆ Investigative
◆ Realistic	◆ Thorough	◆ Inquisitive
◆ Specific	◆ Tactful	◆ Informed
◆ Detailed	◆ Deliberate	◆ Appropriate

Fact Finder is the action mode out of which a person naturally and instinctively probes and gathers information.

A person with a good deal of natural energy in the Fact Finder action mode learns from history, appreciates what did and did not work before, and instinctively gathers information. This person doesn't like to be pushed to do anything until enough information is at hand in order to do the task well.

Appropriateness and thoroughness are key factors for a person with natural energy in the Fact Finder mode. When a Fact Finder is given a task, this person will first stop and gather all the information deemed necessary to get the job done.

Fact Finders are at their best when they can weigh the pros and cons and have time to make a well-thought-out decision.

4

Perspectives of the Fact Finder

The basic perspective of the Fact Finder is on the past, and a person with high intensity in this action mode thinks in terms of tradition and what is and is not appropriate. This person remembers what did and did not work before in similar situations and views a new task from the perspective of what worked before in similar, though not always identical, situations. Background information and thoroughness are important to the Fact Finder.

People who have a good deal of natural energy in the Fact Finder mode typically respond to change by analyzing it and asking "Why?" It isn't that they're against change or that they fight it—they just need to know why the change is necessary, what the change involves, how it relates to what did and didn't work before, and what to expect. Then they need time to think about it. If the change is considered by the Fact Finder to be "appropriate," the Fact Finder typically will be a strong supporter of it.

Without enough information, Fact Finders will become stressed during organizational change. If the company doesn't provide enough information about the change, the Fact Finder either will try to find the answers or listen to rumors.

Fact Finders make an important contribution to organizational change by continuing to ask the question "Why?" and pushing decision-makers to provide enough information to let employees know what will be happening, why the change is important, and what future expectations will be.

Take a Moment

Do you think you have a good deal of natural energy in the Fact Finder action mode? Are you a person who naturally researches and gathers information? who wants things to be appropriate? who frequently asks, "Why?" Review the words and phrases you have underlined or highlighted. Do you think you have a lot of instinctive talent in the Fact Finder action mode? a moderate amount? a lesser amount?

Remember . . .

Each action mode makes important contributions. It's not better to be a Fact Finder than a Follow Thru or a Quick Start than an Implementor. It's just the way people are.

Follow Thru

Follow Thru is the action mode out of which a person naturally and instinctively coordinates and organizes. It is out of this mode that a person is:

- ◆ Efficient
- ◆ Systematic
- ◆ Consistent
- ◆ Methodical
- ◆ Coordinated
- ◆ Disciplined
- ◆ Dependable
- ◆ Theoretical
- ◆ Structured
- ◆ Concise
- ◆ Meticulous
- ◆ Organized

4

A person with a good deal of natural energy in the Follow Thru action mode thinks in terms of patterns and is able to organize almost anything: time, people, desktops, clothes, work, schedules, paper, numbers, budgets, or events. Efficiency and consistency are key factors for a person with high intensity in the Follow Thru action mode.

Follow Thru is the action mode out of which a person naturally and instinctively coordinates and organizes.

When a Follow Thru is given a task and is free to complete it his or her own way, this person will think in terms of organization and order. It's important to this person that everything fits together, is coordinated, and is placed in the proper perspective. When they organize time or work, they do it in terms of what needs to be done first, second, third, and so on. It's also important for the Follow Thru to stay with the original schedule and sequence. Interruptions, unless scheduled or anticipated, usually are stressful.

Follow Thrus are at their best when they can make a decision in a nonrushed, organized manner.

Perspectives of the Follow Thru

The basic perspective of a Follow Thru is integration of past, present, and future. Follow Thrus strive to view things within the context of the whole situation. The person with a high intensity in the Follow Thru mode may outwardly appear to resist change. The person will make comments such as, "Yeah, this may be necessary, but . . ." The yeah-buts often are misinterpreted. It's not that the person actually resists change— just that the Follow Thru wants to know how the change will fit into the overall scheme of things and particularly how it will fit into the system that's already in place. The Follow Thru needs time to think about the change.

Without an agenda of how the change is to take place (what will happen first, next, and so on) and how the change will affect daily routines, the Follow Thru will be stressed during an organizational change. Structure and security are important to Follow Thrus, and if the structure is changed without adequate preparation, threatening job security, this person will be stressed. Because the Follow Thru likes to have his or her day structured—and structured in a consistent way—organizational change can stress the Follow Thru until new patterns are in place. Asking Follow Thrus to do something one way today and a different way tomorrow will be stressful.

Follow Thrus make an important contribution to organizational change by striving to keep balance. Because of their natural instinct to organize, they will strive to bring order out of chaos and find ways to make certain that the things that need doing actually get done.

Take a Moment

Do you think you have a good deal of instinctive energy in the Follow Thru action mode? Are you a person who naturally likes to organize people, papers, numbers, or work? who makes a list of what needs to get done and then follows that list? who frequently says, "'Yeah, but . . . ?" Review the words you've underlined or highlighted. Do you think you have a lot of instinctive talent in the Follow Thru action mode? a moderate amount? a lesser amount?

Quick Start

Quick Start is the action mode out of which a person naturally and instinctively innovates, takes risks, is spontaneous, and quickly moves from project to project. It is out of this action mode that a person is:

- Inventive
- Intuitive
- Flexible
- Fluent

- Imaginative
- Adventurous
- Decisive
- Spontaneous

- Conceptual
- A deal-maker
- A risk-taker
- A promoter

A person with a good deal of natural energy in the Quick Start action mode has many things going on at the same time and may be viewed by others as bouncing off the walls. This person naturally looks for new ways to do things and often is persuasive in promoting an idea, agenda, service, or product.

4

When given a task, the Quick Start naturally begins thinking in terms of innovations and new ways to do what's been done before. Quick Starts work best out of a sense of challenge, and, because he or she typically handles several things at once, appreciates the pressure of deadlines.

Perspectives of the Quick Start

The basic perspective of the Quick Start is that of the future. Quick Starts naturally think in terms of what's ahead and of possibilities. Being instinctively conceptual, they can envision the big picture without getting bogged down with details. They usually are thinking ahead of themselves and others. The freedom to change things is important to the Quick Start.

People who have a good deal of natural energy in the Quick Start action mode respond to change by promoting it. These are the change agents. Quick Starts will be advocates of change, and encourage others to "try it, you'll like it!" A natural risk-taker, the Quick Start is ready to try just about anything that makes sense at the moment and will evaluate it after he or she sees how it all works out.

Quick Start is the action mode out of which a person naturally and instinctively innovates, takes risks, is spontaneous, and quickly moves from project to project.

Quick Starts especially can become stressed during organizational change. They will have a difficult time when they aren't involved in coming up with the new alternatives or when the proposed change doesn't take place quickly enough for them. Quick Starts also will become stressed if the change imposes a structured way of doing things on them.

Quick Starts make an important contribution to organizational change not only by coming up with new ways to approach old tasks, but also by encouraging others to see the benefits of the change. Quick Starts will be the ones who say, "Hey, why not?" or "Let's give it a try," or "What have we got to lose?" Quick Starts thrive in the midst of change. They live for change.

Take a Moment

Do you think you have a good deal of instinctive energy in the Quick Start action mode? Are you a person who is naturally intuitive, flexible, and willing to try different things? who works best under pressure? who frequently asks, "Why not?" Review the words you've underlined or highlighted. Do you think you have a lot of instinctive talent in the Quick Start action mode? a moderate amount? a lesser amount?

Implementor

Implementor is the action mode out of which a person naturally and instinctively works with his or her hands. It is out of this action mode that a person is:

◆ Mechanical	◆ Technical	◆ Tactile
◆ A builder	◆ A fabricator	◆ A crafter
◆ Hands-on	◆ Tangible	◆ A demonstrator

> *Implementor* is the action mode out of which a person naturally and instinctively works with his or her hands.

A person with a good deal of natural energy in the Implementor action mode does things with his or her hands or works with tools and machines, and typically is concerned about the quality of what is produced. This person learns by doing, and naturally is able to visualize space and how best to make use of it.

Remember, the Implementor works with his or her hands. This action mode has nothing to do with "implementing an idea or assignment."

When given a task, the Implementor will stop and visualize what needs to happen. Implementors will gather all the proper tools and materials needed to complete the task and then will set about completing it.

Implementors are at their best when they have time to construct solutions and produce tangible and visual results that meet their standards of quality.

Perspectives of the Implementor

The basic perspective of the Implementor is on the present; he or she thinks in terms of the here and now. Implementors want to make sure that whatever they build will endure, so that the quality of today will be available in the future. They see no need to describe in words what they can present in a model. People with high intensity in the Implementor action mode use props to help them express their ideas to others.

People with a high level of natural energy in the Implementor action mode often aren't as verbal as people with natural energy in the other modes. Since language is conceptual and abstract, to do well with language one also must do well with conceptual and abstract activities. But because Implementors work from the

4

perspective of the present, the specific, and the here and now, they don't approach activities from the perspective of the abstract. It's not that they can't verbally communicate, but that they tend to communicate in specifics. For an implementor, actions truly do speak louder than words.

People who have a good deal of natural energy in the Implementor action mode typically respond to change with a concern for continued quality and continuity. Their concerns tend to focus on the continued opportunity to produce a quality product with the right equipment. If the change involves downgrading the materials or tools used to produce the product, they will resist it. If, on the other hand, the change involves upgrading materials or tools, they will support the change.

Because people with high intensity in the Implementor action mode tend to be nonverbal, the stress they may experience from change isn't always easy to notice. Implementors tend to keep things to themselves; they use few words to communicate their concerns. It's easier for Implementors to talk about personal reactions or feelings when they're working at something with their hands or when they're walking or hiking.

Implementors make an important contribution to organizational change by focusing on the importance of having the right space, the right materials, and the right equipment to produce or provide a quality product.

Take a Moment

Do you think you have a good deal of instinctive energy in the Implementor action mode? Are you a person who naturally works with his or her hands or with machines or tools? who is sometimes nonverbal? who says, "Show me, don't tell me"? Review the words you've underlined or highlighted. Do you think you have a lot of instinctive talent in the Implementor action mode? a moderate amount? a lesser amount?

Combinations

As you've read this information, you may have thought, "I'm not exactly like any one action mode. I seem to be more like a little bit of each, but with more intensity in two of them." You may be right. People have instinctive energy in all four action modes but usually have higher intensities in one or sometimes two of them.

When people have higher levels of natural energy in two action modes, combinations occur. For example, a person may have high intensity in the Quick Start mode as well as the Fact Finder mode. When experiencing organizational change, this person instinctively will promote it and think of even more new ways to get things done. Then the person will stop and ask for more information. If the levels of intensity are fairly equal, the person will go back and forth between supporting the change and wanting to know more about it. It may seem to others that the person sometimes says "Why not?" in the morning and "Why?" in the afternoon.

4

Here's another example. A person with a good deal of natural energy in the Follow Thru and Implementor action modes will respond to organizational change first by wanting to know how it all fits together and then how the change will fit into the existing structure. The person will want some kind of visualization, like a three-dimensional model or a graph or chart. It may seem as if the person says "Yeah, but . . ." one moment and "Show me" the next.

Remember, people have talents in each of the four conative action modes. Most, however, have much stronger levels of energy in one, and sometimes two, of the modes. It's how we are. Some of us naturally gather information, while others naturally organize, innovate, or work with their hands.

Conative Strengths and Organizational Change

People react to organizational change according to their natural instincts—their conative style. That's why some people respond to organizational change one way and others respond another way. Now that you've been introduced to the third part of the mind—the conative part—and have seen how people instinctively and naturally get things done, you know that everyone doesn't react to organizational change in the same way:

◆ **The Fact Finder** instinctively wants enough information about the organizational change to be certain it will be successful, is appropriate to the situation, and is consistent with what's worked before.

◆ **The Follow Thru** instinctively wants the organizational change to be well organized and introduced in a way that helps everyone understand and accept it and will help ensure that everything fits together.

◆ **The Quick Start** will help promote the change and will encourage others to "try it, you'll like it!"

◆ **The Implementor** wants to maintain quality and ensure that the right tools or equipment and adequate space are available to get the job done well.

Take a Moment

Now that you've read through the descriptions of each action mode, you may have a sense of where your natural talents and instincts are. If so, write a brief description in the space below:

_____

_____

_____

If you aren't able to describe you natural talents and instincts after this brief introduction, you may want to read one of Kolbe's books. See page 58 for more information.

Kathy Kolbe defines success as "the freedom to be yourself." When a person is free to be himself or herself, to do things naturally and instinctively, that person is productive, creative, and satisfied. In other words, successful. Work isn't difficult but enjoyable because the person is able to do it in the way that's most natural.

But there's a tradeoff. If you want to be successful, free to be yourself, and respond to organizational change naturally and instinctively, then you must do one more thing. You must acknowledge that others will have different instincts than you do and will naturally respond to organizational change in different ways than you do. We know that in any organization, all people are not just Fact Finders or Quick Starts. There's a variety.

4

As you can see, all conative action modes are helpful when it comes to designing and responding to organizational change. When you *understand* your own natural and instinctive talents, *appreciate* the natural strengths you bring to any situation, and *respect* the natural instincts of others, you set in motion the energy to make change work for you!

Self-Check: Chapter 4 Review

Take a few moments to review this chapter's exercises, then complete your Team Summary:

1. Briefly describe what you think are your own natural instincts:

   _____

   _____

   _____

2. Briefly describe what you have observed may be the natural instincts of the people with whom you work:

   _____

   _____

   _____

3. What are some ways you can support those who have instincts either similar or different to yours?

   _____

   _____

   _____

For more information about conation and the Kolbe Concept™, read either of Kathy Kolbe's books:

The Conative Connection: Uncovering the Link Between Who You Are and How You Perform (Addison Wesley, 1990) and *Pure Instinct: Business' Untapped Resource* (Times Books/Random House, 1993).

Chapter *Five*

Managing the Stress That Comes with Change

Chapter Objective

▶ Master 10 strategies for dealing with the stress of organizational change.

For some people, organizational change results in stress. It may be due to:

♦ A hesitancy to change,

♦ Having to leave your friends from the work unit,

♦ A great deal of change in a short period of time,

♦ New procedures, or

♦ Just plain too much to do with too little time and resources to do it.

You can't make change work for you if you're all stressed out!

Whatever the cause of the stress, there are ways to reduce it.

These 10 strategies have come from people who've tried them and made them work. These people have been where you are now—in the midst of an organizational change—and they've used these strategies to deal with their stress. Not everybody used each strategy, of course, nor should they have. But everyone will find several that fit his or her situation and that can reduce the stress of going through an organizational change. After all, you can't make change work for you if you're all stressed out!

What you'll discover is that these strategies will help you feel better—more energized, more confident, and more able to deal successfully with each day's events!

Strategy 1: Exercise

The single, most helpful way to reduce stress is through exercise! This is the one strategy that is almost universally effective. Everyone benefits from it. And taking advantage of it doesn't have to cost a lot of money.

Sure, there are fitness centers with all kinds of exercise machines. And there are machines you can buy for home use. Those are all nice because they make it easier to stay with your exercise schedule. But they aren't the only options, as others have reported:

■ "When I get stressed, I go for a walk. After 30 minutes, I begin to feel better."

■ "I have some weights at home that I use. After I learned how to use them, I found that a 30-minute workout three times a week does wonders to keep me smiling."

■ "My yard is my exercise. In fact, I realized that I've planned my yard so that I have to work in it at least an hour each evening during the growing seasons. It keeps me stable."

■ "Exercise videos help because they give me some direction, and my neighbor helped me understand how important it is to stretch out and get ready."

It's not how you exercise but the fact that you do it at all that's important. For some, it's running; others swim or participate in group aerobics. I enjoy working in my yard, and when I can't work in my yard, I use my treadmill. The treadmill is in front of the basement TV so I can watch a movie or the news while I exercise. What I've learned is that after about 15 to 20 minutes, I begin to feel better and more relaxed as the endorphins begin to kick in.

5

It's not how you exercise but the fact that you do it at all that's important.

Endorphins? Yes. These are the natural chemicals that our bodies release after a period of exercise. These chemicals reduce stress, relieve pain, and in general, simply make us feel better! Endorphins are what produce the "high" experienced by many joggers and runners. After running for a while, their bodies begin to produce and release endorphins. The result? They feel better.

There are several ways in which our bodies release these natural endorphins, but exercise is the most universal. Exercise for 20 to 30 minutes and you'll naturally feel better because your body will have begun to produce and release endorphins.

Take a Moment

Because exercise is the single most helpful way to reduce stress, it's important that you engage in some kind of regular physical activity—at least three times a week for at least 30 minutes each time. In the space below, describe how you are going to use exercise as a way to help make change work for you:

_____

_____

_____

_____

_____

If you haven't regularly exercised for some time or are over 40, it's important that you have a physical exam before engaging in any strenuous exercise.

Strategy 2: Talk It Out

Some people find it helpful to talk out their stress with someone else. What do they talk about? They vent. They spout. They show their anger. They get their feelings out in the open. The dynamic appears to be this: For some people, it simply helps when they hear themselves say things. When they verbalize their frustration or anger, it becomes easier to deal with it and then to set it aside.

This someone else can be a friend, spouse, parent, child, neighbor, coworker, pastor, rabbi, or professional counselor. The important thing is having someone to talk with. Talking out your stress doesn't necessarily mean that you're looking for agreement or sympathy—just someone who will sit, listen, be genuinely interested in you. The person doesn't even need to say much in return, other than to let you know he or she is listening and is interested in what you have to say. If this person ever has been where you are now, that's often an added plus.

Here's what others have said:

5

- "My sis is a great listener. I can spout off about all I'm going through and get it out of my system."

- "It's interesting the way it works. Once I hear myself say something, it's out in the open where I can deal with it or walk away from it."

- "Usually just telling my significant other about how stressed I am is all it takes. Then I feel better, and it doesn't bother me as much. I'm ready to get back into it the next day."

If you're a person who is helped by talking out your stress, find someone with whom you can talk. You might even find it helpful to "share time"—you listen to the other person for 30 minutes, and then the other person listens to you.

> If you're a person who is helped by talking out your stress, find someone with whom you can talk.

Take a Moment

Many people find it helpful to talk about stress with some-one else. Who are several people with whom you'd be comfortable talking?

_____

_____

_____

_____

Strategy 3: Listen to Music

Music can be like exercise for many people. After listening to whatever kind of music makes them feel good, their bodies also begin to produce endorphins. They naturally feel better. Music can be a great stress-reliever.

What kinds of music are best for relieving stress? There's no universal answer. Some like rock, others find that easy-listening music relaxes them, and still others enjoy classical music, instrumentals, or any kind of vocals. I have my own favorite kinds of music to listen to when I'm stressed; after listening for a while (and sometimes singing along), I always feel better, more energized, and ready to get back to the tasks at hand.

Take a Moment

What kind of music do you enjoy? Have you ever tried listening to music, as a way of reducing stress? If not, then when can you try this strategy?

_____

_____

_____

_____

Strategy 4: Anticipate Times of Stress

By planning ahead and anticipating times of stress, you often can reduce the impact it has. Here's how to do it. Periodically (every week, two weeks, whatever works for you), review your calendar. Project yourself into the future, and identify those times coming up that have the potential for being stressful. When you identify a period of possible high stress, plan for it.

First, admit to yourself that you're going to experience some extra stress so it doesn't catch you by surprise. Second, develop a plan to help you reduce as much of the stress as possible. For example, if you're having a high-stress week at work and you also do the cooking at home, ask for help with the chores at home so you'll have extra energy to deal with the stress at work. Or just plan to eat out.

Third, put your plan into action. When you're in the midst of the high-stress time, stop momentarily to check on how you're doing. Be sure you've made time to do the things that will help you relieve stress—exercising, talking, listening to music. And be sure to get extra sleep. Most people benefit from extra sleep when they're trying to combat stress.

The key is to anticipate times when stress may be high, and then to be ready for them.

> **The key is to anticipate times when stress may be high, and then to be ready for them.**

5

Take a Moment

Set a time when you can project ahead for two weeks, and identify times when the stress level might be high. Identify ways you can prepare for them and even reward yourself after you've made it through the high-stress times.

_____

_____

_____

_____

Strategy 5: Reward Yourself

A strategy I particularly like is to reward myself for my efforts to reduce stress, and I often use it in conjunction with the strategy on planning for times of stress. When I know a stressful time is ahead, I plan for it. Then when it's over, I go out and reward myself. Maybe it's having a dinner out, buying a new tie, or doing something else that's enjoyable for me. A reward can be something as simple as buying some gourmet ice cream or leaving work early. Rewards can be almost anything, and they don't have to cost much.

Rewards give you something to look forward to when the stressful period is over.

What's important is that I plan ahead and tell myself, "You have a real busy couple of days coming up, with more to do than you have time or energy. But you'll get it all done, just like you have in the past. Then, when it's all behind you, you can reward yourself with . . ." Fill in the blank.

Rewards help. They make you feel good about getting something done, and, in the midst of a stressful time, they give you something pleasant to look forward to when it's all over.

Take a Moment

If you've never used the strategy of rewarding yourself, try it. To start, make a list of several things coming up that you want to be sure you will get done well—and the rewards that will help you:

Goal: _____

_____

Reward: _____

_____

Goal: _____

_____

Reward: _____

_____

Strategy 6: Go for a Drive

Some people like to go for a drive. As one person explained, "It settles me down. Driving for an hour out in the country or even on the highway relaxes me." Lots of folks find relaxation behind the wheel.

It's not so much that they're going anywhere, but simply that they're controlling their car—their machine—while they're driving. Although most of us prefer not to drive in high-traffic areas, some report that congested traffic doesn't bother them when they drive to relieve stress. Here's what others have said:

■ "It gives me more to think as I work my way through traffic, and I find that I have lots of patience."

■ "I always have a destination—maybe a park, a nearby river, a favorite shopping center, or a restaurant. When I get there, I spend some time, and then head back. It's a great way to unwind and spend a Saturday afternoon."

Going for a drive is another simple way you can reduce the job stress that comes with organizational change.

5

Take a Moment

Are you a person who likes to go for a drive? If so, briefly describe your favorite drives. If not, are you interested in finding out if driving might help you relieve stress? If you are, describe when and where you could try this strategy:

_____

_____

_____

_____

Strategy 7: Use Moderation

While discussing these stress-reduction strategies with a group of employees whose work unit had just been sold, someone said, "I use the six-pack method of reducing stress." The group laughed. "Yes sir," the employee continued, "I go out and buy a six-pack and by the time it's all gone, I always feel a lot better."

I didn't laugh with the others. Why? Because at one time, the "six-pack method" also was my primary way of reducing stress. It took me several months to realize that:

◆ It was costing me a good deal of money.

◆ I always had a terrible headache when I woke up the next morning.

◆ Others really didn't think I was very pleasant or funny.

◆ I was using "the six-pack method" more and more often.

◆ The stress always was still there the next day.

With the help of some understanding friends, I set that particular strategy aside.

A very effective strategy to replace it is simply to use moderation in just about everything: in drinking, in eating, in sleeping, and yes, even in exercise. Too much exercise, especially if you're not already in shape, can create more problems than it solves.

Take a Moment

Think about your lifestyle. In what areas could you benefit from moderation? List them in the space below:

_____

_____

_____

_____

Strategy 8: Use Your Conative Strengths

The previous chapter, "Why People React Differently to Change " described conation and conative strengths. It's essential reading if you are to understand and use one very important stress-reduction strategy: Use your conative strengths!

One of the reasons we can become stressed in the first place is that we weren't given the chance to use our natural energy in the action area of our strongest conative instincts. When we become stressed, one way to reduce the stress is to do the things that come naturally to us.

> **When we become stressed, one way to reduce the stress is to do the things that come naturally to us.**

◆ **Fact Finders,** for example, become stressed when they don't have all the information they need. One way they can reduce their stress is to do some probing, researching, and information gathering, such as reading a book, a magazine, watching a TV documentary, enjoying a mystery, or taking time to read the newspaper without interruption. Many Fact Finders report that the more stress they're under, the more books they read. If you think you have a lot of natural Fact-Finder instinct and are under stress, use your conative instinct: Do that research you've been meaning to get to, read those reports that have been piling up on your desk, catch up on your professional journals, or just read whatever it is you enjoy reading.

◆ **Follow Thrus** become stressed when the organizational structure is changed or is in limbo, when they can't see how things will all fit together, or when there's no sense of closure or completion to anything. One way they can reduce their stress is to organize something, like their office, their desk, or a filing cabinet. One person told me he had the best-organized office in the department, as well as the best-organized closet at home. He reviewed his project files and reorganized them to better fit his future needs. At home, he organized his clothes by season and by color within each season, and then by whether they were for work, dress, or casual wear. If you think you have a good deal of Follow Thru instinct, make use of your natural talent. When you're stressed, organize your office or your desk or whatever needs your special talent at keeping things in order. Bring something to completion.

5

69

◆ **Quick Starts** can become stressed during organizational change when the change doesn't occur fast enough or when not enough new things are taking place to utilize their natural energy. When that happens, Quick Starts can energize themselves by starting something new or by coming up with a new way to do something that isn't being done as well as it could be. If you think you have a good deal of Quick Start instinct, make use of your natural talent. When you're stressed, go to work on a new project, take a look at an old problem to see if you can come up with a new solution, or identify a project that needs your innovative talents.

◆ **Implementors** become stressed when there's no physical action, when they fear that the quality of what's being produced is about to be compromised, or when the quality of the tools they need to be productive may be sacrificed. When this happens, Implementors need to do something physical or work with their hands. If you think you have a good deal of Implementor instinct, make use of your natural talent. When you're stressed, use your talents to build or repair something, work in the yard, wash the car, go for a walk, cross-stitch, lift weights, cook, or whatever you find enjoyable that uses your Implementor instincts. Implementors can reduce stress by doing something physical.

Whatever your conative instincts, you can use them to help reduce stress.

Whatever your conative instincts, you can use them to help reduce stress. To deny them or "go against the grain" will only add to your frustration.

Take a Moment

Indicate what seem to be the Kolbe Conative Action Modes™ in which you have the most strengths.

_____

_____

_____

Take a Moment

What ways can you make use of your conative instincts to help reduce stress?

_____

_____

_____

Strategy 9: Challenge Your Mind-Set

This strategy has to do with mind-set—the way you think. Psychologist Albert Ellis pointed out many years ago that unless an event is life-threatening, it's stressful only if we choose to let it be stressful. In other words, it's how we interpret an event that determines our reactions to it—not the event itself.

For example, imagine that you've had to work 20 minutes beyond your usual break time for lunch. Being 20 minutes late for lunch is the event. How you interpret that event determines your reaction to it. If you say something like, "Well, I don't like being late because I'm hungry, but it's no big deal," then your reaction will reflect that it's no big deal to you. You'll go ahead and simply be 20 minutes late for lunch.

On the other hand, if you interpret that event and say to yourself something like, "This is terrible. It shouldn't have happened, and I'm very angry at the imposition," then your reaction will reflect that interpretation. You'll be angry, and because of your anger, you'll probably get indigestion when you finally do eat lunch. In both examples, the event is the same, but the reactions are greatly different. What makes all the difference is how you interpret the event—your mind-set.

During organizational change, you have the opportunity to challenge your mind-set. Your interpretation of the change will determine your reaction to it. If you say something like, "This is terrible, the worst thing that's ever happened to me, and I'll never get over it," then that's probably what will happen. You

5

Your interpretation of the change will determine your reaction to it.

71

probably never will get over it. The organizational change will have an impact on you for a long, long time. You'll waste a lot of energy being angry over something that was beyond your control.

What is within your control, however, is your mind-set. You could, on the other hand, interpret the event like this: "Gee, this isn't the most fun I've ever had, and I'll be glad when it's all over, but for now I'm going to make the most of it." Then your reaction probably would be to make the most of the organizational change, and you'd likely get your work done and remain someone who others enjoy working with. Yes, you'd experience some stress, but not enough to make the job unbearable. And you'd get over it.

How you interpret an event is largely up to you. One strategy for dealing with any stress that comes from organizational change is to keep track of how you interpret events and to challenge your mind-set. Make the most of what happens!

How you interpret an event is largely up to you.

Take a Moment

Briefly describe how you've been interpreting the current organizational change:

_____

_____

_____

If your interpretation of the organizational change results in negative reactions to the change, how can you challenge your mind-set and adjust your interpretation so you can make change work for you?

_____

_____

_____

Strategy 10: Laugh

Laughter is one of the best stress-relievers there is—in fact, it's a very close second to exercise! Some people may even rank it first. Laughing gets the whole body and mind working. Muscles relax and endorphins (yes, those endorphins again!) begin to flow. Researchers have found that people in hospitals who watched comedy TV shows or funny movies and laughed out loud recovered faster than those who didn't. So laugh a lot!

Maybe it's a funny movie (I'm hooked on the Pink Panther series of Peter Sellers movies), a funny TV show, a visit to a comedy club, or just a talk with someone who makes you laugh—whatever makes you laugh will help. And it even will help those who don't think it will help!

> **Laughter is one of the best stress-relievers there is.**

Humorist C.W. Metcalf makes a career out of teaching people how to laugh. He uses his suggestions in his own life, too. One of the things that helps him relax and laugh is putting on a red clown nose as he drives home from work. "It's hard to take yourself too seriously when you're wearing a clown nose," Metcalf says, "and besides, you see some awfully funny reactions from a lot of people."

5

You don't have to wear a clown nose to laugh. But if it helps, give it a try. Just remember that laughing is one of the best stress-relievers there is!

Take a Moment

What makes you laugh? What do you think is funny? What are things you can do to help you laugh?

_____

_____

_____

_____

Still More Strategies

Are these the only stress-relievers there are? No, far from it! There are lots of others, and without discussing any of them in detail, here are 10 more:

1. Going for a walk—around the block, in a park, or along a river

If you're going to make change work for you, you have to deal with stress in positive ways.

2. Sitting and watching a sunrise, a sunset, a lake, or the ocean

3. Volunteering—helping others deal with their lives

4. Shopping—whether just looking or buying

5. Reading a good book

6. Watching a movie or a play

7. Participating in a sport—or just being an active spectator or fan

8. Sexual activity—a great way to relax

9. Working at a hobby—stained glass, cross-stitch, cooking, stamp collecting, whatever

10. Reflection, meditation, or prayer

Remember, stress works on you and gets you down. If you're going to make change work for you, you have to deal with stress in positive ways—and it all begins with the commitment to do something instead of nothing.

Self-Check: Chapter 5 Review

Circle True or False for the statements below.

1. True or False?
   Exercise is the single most helpful stress-reliever.

2. True or False?
   There are many things people can do to relieve the stress that results from organizational change.

3. True or False?
   Some people find it helpful to "talk it out" with someone they can trust.

4. True or False?
   Using a person's conative instincts is a natural way to get reenergized.

5. True or False?
   There are so many ways to reduce stress that it is self-defeating to do nothing instead of something.

6. True or False?
   If a person reacts negatively to the organizational change, it might help if the person challenges his or her mind-set.

7. True or False?
   Managing stress is important to make change work for you.

If you marked all of the above items True, pat yourself on the back! You're well on your way to reducing any stress that's a result of organizational change. You're learning how to make change work for you!

In the space below, describe at least three different ways you can reduce any stress you may experience as a result of organizational or personal change.

1. _____

2. _____

3. _____

Chapter *Six*

How Work Teams React to Organizational Change

Chapter Objectives

▶ Explain how work teams react to organizational change.

▶ Recognize why some employees leave when change takes place.

▶ Identify how you can help your work team deal with organizational change.

When you know and understand how work teams react to organizational change, these reactions won't blindside you or catch you by surprise.

In Chapter 4, you learned how individuals can vary widely in their reactions to organizational change. When it comes to groups of employees, however, there seems to be more consistency. What we've learned over the years is that the way a group of employees reacts to organizational change is fairly predictable. It doesn't seem to make much difference whether the "group of employees" is a small work team or a larger work unit or even an entire department. Sure, there are variations, but the reaction pattern generally is consistent.

When you know and understand how work teams react to organizational change, these reactions won't blindside you or catch you by surprise. You'll be able to make change work for you, and you'll also be able to help the team collectively deal with the change in an effective manner.

You'll understand that teams of any size or description go through these five stages: positioning, confusion, clarification, focus, and acceptance. These changes are normal, so there's nothing wrong with your work team if it exhibits these reactions.

After the announcement of change, work teams go through a reaction pattern that looks like this:

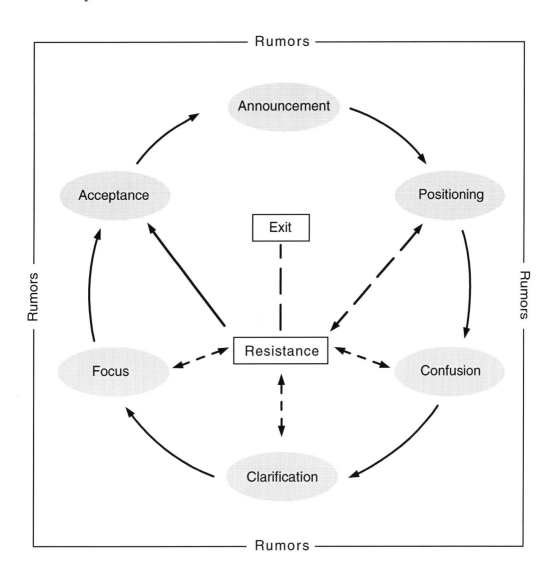

6

What we've learned is that each work unit will go through each stage. Work units may vary in how long they remain in one stage or another, however, depending on the makeup of the unit and on how well the change is being managed. And throughout all of this, there is the ever-present reality of rumors.

Setting the Stage: Rumors and the Announcement

Even before a formal announcement is made about any reorganization or change in the company, there will be rumors. Some will be fairly accurate, and others will be totally wrong. Some people will listen to the rumors, particularly the gloom-and-doom predictions, and others will pay them little attention.

How do rumors get started? Somehow, groups of employees begin to realize that some kind of change is about to take place, even before any formal announcement is made. Just by watching the actions of company managers they can sense that a change is coming. And then rumors run rampant.

Most rumors are wrong.

But most rumors are wrong.

Because of rumors, the company's formal announcement usually isn't a total surprise. The specifics of the announcement may be a surprise, but in general, earlier discussions among employees will have anticipated much of what the announcement will say. The announcement is quickly followed by the first stage, Positioning.

Take a Moment

Think about a recent change in your company that involved your work team, and respond to the following questions:

Were there rumors?

_____

_____

How accurate were the rumors?

_____

_____

How much attention did others give to the rumors?

_____

_____

6

Stage 1: Positioning

The formal announcement is quickly followed by a time of *positioning.* Work units stop, step back, and take an initial position on the announced change. Within a company, there even may be some jockeying as various work teams attempt to position themselves for what each perceives to be the best response. These positions will vary from unit to unit and are determined by the key influencers within each team.

When the organizational change involves only a single team, there still is jockeying for position among the team members to see who will influence the total group. Whoever wins will set the stage for how others in the group will respond to the change. Though individuals will vary in their particular positions, each work team typically comes to its own collective stand about the organizational change.

> During the positioning stage, work units stop, step back, and take an initial position on the announced change.

These positions usually fall into the following categories:

◆ **Relief**
For some work teams, there is a sigh of relief—as if collectively the group says, "Finally, at last we know what's going to take place." Many people don't like to live on the question mark, and rumors can be unsettling. For these work units, it's easier to deal with the known—even if they don't like it—than it is to deal with the unknown.

◆ **Anger**
For some work teams, the position toward the announcement is one of anger. It's as if the group collectively says, "How dare you do this to us! We're upset, angry, and mad, and somehow we'll get even." The anger can manifest itself in lack of cooperation, decline in productivity, and general doom-and-gloom behavior by the unit as a whole.

◆ **Anxiety**
Some work teams respond to the announcement with anxiety. "What great tragedy will happen next?" they seem to ask. It's as if they're looking back over their shoulders all the time, waiting for something else to happen. Because of their anxiety, they're unable to see anything positive in the announcement.

◆ **Wait and see**
Some work teams position themselves with the cautious "let's wait and see how this works out" response. They typically don't try to block whatever change is taking place, nor do they fight it. But they aren't necessarily enthusiastic supporters, either. A work unit that positions itself with a wait-and-see attitude still can be influenced by others— other work units or company supervisors and managers. The successful influencer is the one with the most appealing message.

◆ **Opportunity**

Many work teams position themselves to see primarily the opportunities that come with organizational change! They support the change, and tend to talk among themselves and with other teams about its potential benefits. A work unit that supports the change can help other units modify their initial positions, particularly if it's well-liked and respected and perceived as influential with the new decision-makers.

Regardless of its size, a work team's first reaction to an announcement of organizational change is to position itself in terms of its response. And the way the change is announced—and the way influencers react to the announcement—can sway work teams either way.

Take a Moment

Think back to the recent change that involved your work team (or another recent organizational change), and respond to the following questions:

How did your work team position itself?

_____

_____

Did other work teams position themselves similarly or differently?

_____

_____

Can you identify influencers within your own work team? Within other work teams?

_____

_____

6

Stage 2: Uncertainty

Positioning is quickly followed by *uncertainty*. In many instances, uncertainty about what the announcement really means sets in before the end of the day. People ask questions like:

◆ Will it have an impact on me?

◆ Will I still have a job?

◆ Will my friends still have jobs?

◆ Will I have new coworkers? a new boss?

◆ Will I have to move to a new location?

◆ Who's making decisions?

◆ What do these decision-makers know about me?

◆ Who has power?

◆ Who no longer has power?

◆ Will I have to take a cut in pay?

> **In any organizational change, it's not possible for the announcement to include all of the specific details.**

Uncertainty is fueled by not having answers to questions like these. People need to understand that in any organizational change, it's not possible for the announcement to include all of the specific details and address all the implications of what the change really means. Sometimes even the key decision-makers don't know what all of the implications will be. It just takes time to work everything out, and during that time, there will be uncertainty.

I grew up with the notion that all executives, company presidents, and top-level managers knew everything. They were wise. They were leaders. And they didn't make mistakes. Not so!

In any organizational change, management always contributes to the uncertainty. Sometimes it's not so much uncertainty as it is confusion. This is the time when decision-makers are trying to deal with all aspects of the change. They may seem to say one thing one day and come back the next and say something completely different. Nothing seems consistent.

For some, this time of uncertainty is just too much. They either decide they don't have to put up with it, or they decide that it's more than they can tolerate. They begin to resist and might ultimately exit. For people who don't necessarily like change, this time of uncertainty can be very difficult.

Take a Moment

Think about the recent change you have experienced (or some other recent organizational change):

Was there a good deal of uncertainly, even some confusion?

_____

_____

Was management always consistent or always ready with answers?

_____

_____

Were there some who exited the company?

_____

_____

What did others say about this time of uncertainty?

_____

_____

What did you say about this time of uncertainty?

_____

_____

6

Stage 3: Clarification

Uncertainty finally gives way to a sense of *clarification*. Employees begin to find answers, and management becomes more consistent. Employees begin to understand who has power and who doesn't, and what decision-makers think of their work teams. They begin to understand their role in the organizational change.

Not only is the organizational structure becoming more clear, but the expectations of the employees also are being clarified. If a new "company culture" is being promoted, employees begin to understand what that new culture is all about.

Uncertainty and even confusion now are being replaced by clarification. Clarification can deal with:

◆ Expectations

◆ Leadership roles

◆ Procedures

◆ Benefits

◆ Promotions

◆ Employee downsizing

◆ Pay procedures

Each work team that goes through organizational change will have its own areas for which it seeks clarification.

Each work team that goes through organizational change will have its own areas for which it seeks clarification.

How long does it take to go from uncertainty to clarification? It depends. If top management understands change and how to manage it, it may not take long. Management will understand how difficult it is for employees to deal with uncertainty, and will work hard to clarify roles, procedures, and expectations as quickly as possible.

If management helps employees understand and deal with organizational change, clarification will take place more rapidly. Then employees will be able to understand their reactions and what it will take to make change work for them. They'll also understand how they can help make the change process more productive.

Take a Moment

Think about the recent change you experienced (or some other recent organizational change):

How long before there were areas of clarification?

_____

_____

Are there still areas or issues that need clarification? If so, list them.

_____

_____

6

Stage 4: Focus

Clarification is followed by a time of *focus*. The questions and issues raised during the periods of confusion and clarification have been resolved. In other words, the direction has been set, and now focus is present.

> **Focus is the time when management knows where it's going and how it's going to get there.**

Focus is the time when management knows where it's going and how it's going to get there. If there have been changes in leadership, the new leaders are in place and in charge. Their visions of the company and its direction are clear. These visions may be the same as they were before, or they may be different. But there is no uncertainty as to what they are, and management shares the visions—the focus—with employees.

The expectations for employees also are clear. People know their roles, what is and is not expected of them, and how they are to get things done. Meeting these new expectations may involve a considerable amount of change—or not much at all. Employees may or may not like the new focus. But at least the direction has been set: There's no more living on the question mark.

Take a Moment

Think about the recent change that involved your work team (or some other recent organizational change):

Has your work team reached the focus stage yet? If so, how long did it take from the time of the announcement?

_____

_____

If not, identify the areas in which there still is uncertainty or in which clarification is just beginning to take place:

_____

_____

Stage 5: Acceptance

Acceptance is the final stage. It is the time when employees accept the organizational change, and react in one of three ways:

◆ **Acceptance with enthusiasm**
Employees who accept all aspects of the organizational change with enthusiasm now are energized by what has taken place. They like the new direction, the new procedures, and the new leaders. They buy into the new challenges, and their work reflects their new enthusiasm.

◆ **Acceptance with caution**
Employees who accept the organizational change with caution still have the "wait and see" attitude. They may like some aspects of the change, but hesitate to endorse all of it. They may like some of the new direction, but can't bring themselves to enthusiastically support it. They decide to wait and see what happens. In the meantime, they get their work done, usually within the range of expectation but seldom better than that. Because people don't like to live on the question mark, these employees will either move on to acceptance with enthusiasm or acceptance with indifference.

◆ **Acceptance with indifference**
Employees who accept change with indifference do so because "it's only a job." Their enthusiasm for their work may wane, their willingness to do extra work may be nonexistent, and they may just barely accomplish enough to keep from being fired. They may not intentionally sabotage what the work unit and the company are trying to accomplish, but they certainly don't add anything to the workplace environment. They are neither fun to be with nor fun to work with. Some will stay in this stage until they retire; they're the people about whom others say, "He retired several months ago, but he just hasn't left yet." They either will move on to another job, exit, get fired for poor performance, or, sometimes, move to acceptance with caution and maybe even acceptance with enthusiasm.

There is yet another way in which work teams can react to organizational change: resistance and exit.

> **Employees who accept all aspects of the organizational change with enthusiasm now are energized by what has taken place.**

6

Resistance and Exit

Just as rumors surround the reaction patterns of work units that go through change, there also is the dynamic of resistance and exit. You'll notice that there are broken lines leading to the resistance box in the center of the Organization Change Reaction Cycle illustration on page 77. At every stage, individual employees, and sometimes entire work teams, can move into resistance.

Resistance can take many different forms, including:

◆ Reacting negatively to all that is said and done.

◆ Refusing to go along with new policies and/or procedures.

◆ Becoming difficult to work with.

◆ Becoming sullen or silent.

◆ Attempting to convince others to resist the changes.

Those in resistance will either exit on their own or return to the usual reaction pattern.

One of two things will happen to those in resistance: Either they will exit on their own, or they'll return to the usual reaction pattern. Ultimately, unless they exit, they'll move on to some form of acceptance.

Whew! It took a lot of pages to describe what takes place when work teams go through organizational change. But now you know. And since you also know that it's a normal reaction pattern, you won't worry that something's wrong with your team if it experiences a time of confusion or clarification as it moves toward acceptance. It's normal.

With this new knowledge, you now can make change work for you by helping your team complete each stage.

Helping Your Team Reach Acceptance

Here are five things your team can do that will smooth the way to acceptance:

1. Don't listen to rumors. They usually aren't true and often do little more than raise the anxiety level of your coworkers. The best way to deal with rumors is to leave them alone or to make fun of them. Encourage your coworkers to do the same.

2. Talk about the Organizational Change Reaction Cycle with your coworkers. Help the group keep track of the stage you're in. And remember that decision-makers don't always have all the answers and that confusion is a normal part of organizational change.

3. Encourage your team members to view change as opportunity. Talk about the opportunities the change will bring, and help others see the potential for new opportunities, too.

4. Encourage your team members to be upbeat and to keep a positive attitude. The best way to do this is to be upbeat yourself—to smile, be positive, and to step up and assist whenever and wherever you're needed. Demonstrate that organizational change isn't the end of your world.

5. Be supportive to others. By encouraging your team members to deal effectively with organizational change, you're actually making change work for you!

6

Self-Check: Chapter 6 Review

Review your notes from this chapter and the illustration on page 77.

1. Think through how your work team has reacted. Was it similar to the illustration? Were there some differences?

   _____

   _____

   _____

2. Would you illustrate your work unit's reaction to organizational change as a circle? square? roller coaster? triangle? some other shape?

   _____

   _____

   _____

3. On the next page, draw your own illustration of how your work team has reacted to the organizational change.

Chapter *Seven*

How Work Teams Can Survive Downsizing

Chapter Objective

▶ Follow 10 steps to survive a downsizing.

Downsizings are a common part of today's workplace as companies struggle to remain competitive in a rapidly changing marketplace. As the marketplace changes, companies must make adjustments in order to remain profitable or competitive. Downsizing is the present strategy of choice. We may not like it, but that's the way it is. What should you do if your company decides to downsize?

How to Survive a Downsizing

You don't have to just sit back and watch a downsizing happen. There are a number of things you can do that will make a difference. In other words, you can be part of the solution instead of part of any problem. If you decide to make change work for you, you'll find that you're a good deal more satisfied with your job and that your coworkers appreciate your positive attitude.

Here are 10 action steps you can take to help you and your work team survive a downsizing:

◆ **Action 1: Keep a positive attitude.**
There's nothing as discouraging as someone with a sour, negative attitude, who only talks about the bad things taking place. That kind of dark mood can quickly spread to others. However, the reverse also is true. There's nothing as helpful as a person with a positive attitude, who is cheerful, easy to work with, and pleasant to be around. One of the most helpful things you can do for your friends on your work team is to remain positive—to look for new opportunities, new visions, and new goals.

> **Look for new opportunities, new visions, and new goals.**

◆ **Action 2: Be a friend.**
You may have several good friends who exit as part of the downsizing. One action you can take is to remain their friend. Just because they leave doesn't mean you can't continue to do things together or enjoy each other's company. Besides, they probably will want to know what is happening within the company and who is doing what.

Being a friend can include sharing information (like the material presented later in this chapter on the Deems Job-Loss Reaction Cycle™), listening when the person needs to vent, and continuing to include the person in social activities.

7

> If your total work team finds that it is having trouble dealing with the down-sizing, ask your team manager for some help from the company.

◆ **Action 3: Ask for help if you need it.**
If you're having trouble dealing with the fact that you have a job while some of your friends don't, ask for help. Many communities have special centers to help people deal with job loss, and they can help "survivors," too.

If your total work team finds that it is having trouble dealing with the downsizing, ask your team manager for some help from the company. Don't be embarrassed by asking for help. It shows a sense of maturity, self-awareness, and the commitment to make change work for you.

◆ **Action 4: Be supportive of new people.**
In any downsizing, there almost always are some personnel changes. You may find yourself with a new supervisor, new department manager, or new division executive. You even may find yourself with some new people in your work unit.

Give these new people a chance. Listen to what they have to say. Help them get acquainted with your work team's routines and procedures. Help them get acquainted with the people in your work group and in other groups with which you interact. Give them a chance, and be supportive. Everyone involved will appreciate your positive, upbeat approach.

◆ **Action 5: Remind yourself that managers are human, too.** Not all decision-makers are monsters—even if they appear that way sometimes. They are human, too. They make mistakes. They don't like doing things that negatively affect others' lives. They'd rather build than tear down. So give them a break.

◆ **Action 6: Do your job.**
The stress on everyone is high during a downsizing, and there's a tendency for productivity and quality to decline. However, a drop in productivity or quality only adds to the stress. You'll find it easier on yourself and your coworkers if you maintain your energy level and get your job done— accurately and on time.

◆ **Action 7: Make a commitment.**
Decide that you're going to make change work for you, and encourage others to make the same commitment! Once you decide to make change work for you, you'll find that surviving a downsizing is much easier. Sometimes it takes extra energy, but your work unit wants to be part of the solution—not part of the problem.

◆ **Action 8: Remind yourself what it was like before the downsizing.**
It's an interesting dynamic that, in the midst of organizational change, employees tend to forget all the things they didn't like before the downsizing. So stop and remind yourself what it was like before the downsizing. After all, you may find that you like things a whole lot better now than before.

> Remember that businesses sometimes have to make hard decisions, and sometimes those decisions aren't ones we like.

◆ **Action 9: Don't get caught with an unrealistic sense of guilt.**
Sometimes remaining employees experience guilt feelings because they still have jobs and their friends do not. This is an unrealistic and nonsensical guilt. It doesn't do remaining employees any good, and it doesn't do those who've left any good, either. Remember that businesses sometimes have to make hard decisions, and sometimes those decisions aren't ones we like.

If you find you're having unrealistic guilt feelings because you still have a job, seek help. You'll help yourself and will be a more supportive friend to those who left.

◆ **Action 10: Take time to understand the Deems Job-Loss Reaction Cycle™.**
This is a normal reaction cycle experienced by those who go through job loss. Everybody who goes through job loss goes through the cycle. Even employees who remain after a downsizing go through the cycle. When you understand the cycle and accept the reactions as normal, you are making change work for you.

7

The Deems Job-Loss Reaction Cycle™

Employees who remain after a downsizing go through a reaction pattern.

Employees who remain after a downsizing go through a reaction pattern in much the same way as those whose jobs were eliminated. The only difference is the level of intensity. People who lose their jobs typically react to job loss with greater intensity than those who remain and who then watch their friends and coworkers exit.

I first identified this cycle in the early 1980s, as my work turned to helping those who went through job loss. Prior to that, my work had involved helping people deal with terminal illness or the death of a loved one. When my work shifted to helping those who had gone through job loss, it was obvious that there were some major differences in the reaction cycle.

As my research base expanded, it was clear that there was a separate and distinct reaction cycle for job loss. What I've since learned is that people don't go through this job-loss cycle in a neat, linear, sequential way. Instead, as the arrows indicate, it's an up-and-down process. People can go through the cycle several times in one day, or they can become stuck in one stage for a while. Ultimately, most people reach Acceptance and stay there.

The reaction cycle for people who lose their jobs, as well as for those who remain after a downsizing, looks like this:

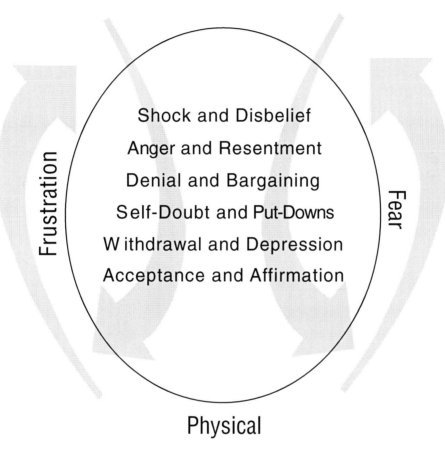

Survivors (employees who remain after a downsizing) go through this cycle in an atmosphere of fear, frustration, and physical reactions. There is the fear that it will happen to them next, or that salaries will be reduced, or . . . (people tend to fill in their own blanks). There also is lots of frustration as survivors have to pick up the work previously done by those who left, as well as deal with organizational changes that are part of any downsizing. The frustration also extends to concerns about one's job future, and just having to deal with change.

There also are physical reactions, and it's common for work teams that survive a downsizing to experience an increase in colds and flulike symptoms. For some, there are even more complicated physical reactions, such as ulcers and colitis. Still others may need medication to help them deal with the stress.

Within this environment, people who survive a downsizing go through the following stages:

1. **Shock/Disbelief**
   The first immediate reaction is that of shock and disbelief. Even though there may have been rumors about the downsizing, people still aren't prepared—and the final word, the actual announcement, results in shock and disbelief. For most employees, this stage lasts only a few minutes to a few hours.

2. **Anger/Resentment**
   Anger and resentment quickly follow. Maybe the anger is directed toward the manager who made the announcement or to key decision-makers or even to "the company" in general. The anger is caused by many reactions: anger that jobs have to be eliminated, anger over who is and who is not exiting, anger over the need for organizational change, and on and on.

   What we've learned is that if this anger isn't dealt with and set aside, it can consume people. Work units that remain must be certain that they have worked through their anger and put it into perspective, or the anger could keep them from doing what's in their own best interest.

3. **Denial/Bargaining**
   The remaining work units have a tendency to do a lot of denial and bargaining after a downsizing has been announced. Sometimes they try to fool themselves and deny the reality of the downsizing. "They'll change their minds," is often heard, along with "Just wait, they'll see how those folks are needed and call them back." But because most downsizings take place only after decision-makers have considered many alternatives, they are a reality. The chances of a callback typically are slim to none.

Bargaining often is very subtle. Productivity often increases after an announcement of a plant or office closing or a downsizing. It's as if people say to themselves, "Maybe if we work harder, they'll see how much all of us are needed . . ."

4. **Self-Doubt/Put-Downs**
   Work units often feel that they are the specific reason for the downsizing. "If only . . ." is often heard spoken out loud, and more often unspoken. At this point, self-confidence wavers and employees wonder if they have what it takes to be successful in today's competitive marketplace. What is needed to counteract this dynamic is a reminder of all that they have accomplished. Individual employees need to be reminded of their contributions.

5. **Withdrawal/Depression**
   At some point, work units withdraw from others, particularly from management. Employees will seem quiet, almost sullen. Individual work units may withdraw within their own department, and even seem to exclude other work groups. Sometimes this withdrawal and depression are a result of feeling guilty over being the survivors, those who still have jobs. This stage is similar to the anger stage. If it's not dealt with and things aren't put into perspective, it can consume people. Any reactions of guilt over still having a job need to be dealt with, and feelings of depression need to be confronted. Sometimes entire work units can benefit from meeting with community specialists.

6. **Acceptance/Affirmation**
   This is the goal. This is the stage at which work units are able to say something like:

■ Sure didn't enjoy this. Would have been easier if it hadn't happened. But it has, and we're dealing with it. We accept the reality of the situation, and know that there is lots of change taking place, and we affirm that we have skills and much to contribute now and in the future.

7

A work unit has reached acceptance and affirmation when it can:

♦ Talk about the downsizing and realistically assess the results.

♦ Accept its own reactions to the job loss experienced by others.

♦ Affirm that it has skills and strengths.

♦ Accept the changing workplace and the need for continued change.

♦ Affirm that it knows how, or will find out how, to remain productive in the changing workplace.

♦ Affirm that it makes contributions.

Sometimes it just takes time for people to reach, and stay, in acceptance and affirmation.

Over the years, we've learned that:

♦ People who remain after a downsizing go through this cycle just as those who exited, but usually not to the same extent.

♦ It is an up-and-down cycle.

♦ People can be in acceptance and affirmation and then suddenly find themselves back in anger or some other stage for awhile, before returning to acceptance.

♦ Because this is a normal reaction, there isn't anything wrong with people who go through this cycle; they're normal.

If your work unit is going through a downsizing, you've already begun to go through the cycle. Now that you understand what happens to people who go through job loss and what happens to people who remain in their jobs, you can more effectively make change work for you!

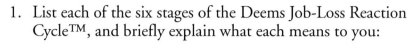

Self-Check: Chapter 7 Review

1. List each of the six stages of the Deems Job-Loss Reaction Cycle™, and briefly explain what each means to you:

   a. _____

   _____

   b. _____

   _____

   c. _____

   _____

   d. _____

   _____

   e. _____

   _____

   f. _____

   _____

2. Identify three survival strategies you can use, and describe them below.

   a. _____

   _____

   b. _____

   _____

   c. _____

   _____

7

Chapter *Eight*

Your Action Plan for Making Change Work

Chapter Objectives

▶ Assess your understanding of how to make change work for you.

▶ Review the A.C.T strategy.

▶ Develop your own personal plan for action.

My father used to tell a story about taking action:

■ As I got out of my car at the ranch house, I could hear the rancher's dog howling as if in pain. I looked around, and there was the dog, sitting by the barn, howling and making a terrible noise. As the rancher and I talked about the weather and sports, the dog just kept howling. Finally I asked, "What's the matter with your dog?"

The rancher looked at me and looked at the dog and finally replied, "Well, I 'magine he's sittin' on a cactus spike, and he'd rather sit and holler than get up an' move."

When it comes to dealing with change, it seems there are those who would rather sit around and gripe than do something about it. You, however, are someone who wants to do something about it! Otherwise, you wouldn't have reached this chapter on putting it all into action.

In this chapter, you will be guided through a brief assessment process to see if there are chapters or sections you need to reread. Then you will be introduced to the A.C.T. approach to change. Your final activity will be to design a plan for action that makes change work for you!

Assess Your Understanding of Change

Working your way through the assessment exercise below will help you clarify and strengthen your insight into change and how to make it work for you. Take time now to complete the assessment. Afterward, you may find that you want to go back and reread certain chapters or selected pages. That's okay—it means that you want to get the full benefit from this book. Often one of the best ways to really understand something new is to reread the information and think about it again.

After reading this book and completing the interactive exercises, I can . . .

> Often one of the best ways to really understand something new is to reread the information and think about it again.

Topic	Degree of proficiency				
	1	2	3	4	5
1. Describe how we are what we are because of change.	1	2	3	4	5
2. Explain how organizational change that affects relationships often is the most difficult kind of change to go through.	1	2	3	4	5
3. Describe how organizational change will continue at a rapid pace.	1	2	3	4	5

(If you have any questions on the subject of what we know about change, please reread Chapter 2.)

4. Describe at least five different strategies to make change work for me.	1	2	3	4	5
5. Explain at least three strategies I can use today to help make change work for me.	1	2	3	4	5
6. Ask "the consultant's question."	1	2	3	4	5

8

(If you need more information on strategies to help make change work for you, reread Chapter 3.)

Topic	Degree of proficiency				
	1	**2**	**3**	**4**	**5**
7. Explain the concept of conation and how each person's conative instincts affect how people react to organizational change.	1	2	3	4	5
8. Describe four major ways in which people naturally react to change in different ways.	1	2	3	4	5
9. Identify my major natural way of responding to organizational change.	1	2	3	4	5

(If you need more information on the different ways people naturally react to change, reread Chapter 4.)

Topic					
10. Identify at least five ways to effectively manage stress as a result of going through change.	1	2	3	4	5
11. Explain at least three strategies I can use today to help me more effectively manage the stress of organizational change.	1	2	3	4	5
12. Explain how and why exercise is the single most productive way to effectively manage stress.	1	2	3	4	5
13. Explain what endorphins are and how exercise, music, and laughter release them into our systems.	1	2	3	4	5

(If you need more information on managing stress, please reread Chapter 5.)

Topic	Degree of proficiency				
	1	2	3	4	5
14. Explain the five stages of how work units react to organizational change.	1	2	3	4	5
15. Explain how some employees will, as they work through these stages, move to resistance and even exit.	1	2	3	4	5
16. Describe why some employees exit shortly after the announcement of organizational change is made.	1	2	3	4	5

(If you need more information on how work units react to change, please reread Chapter 6.)

17. Tell someone else about the normal reaction cycle that remaining employees experience after a downsizing.	1	2	3	4	5
18. Describe at least three ways remaining employees can help exiting employees after a downsizing.	1	2	3	4	5

8

(If you need more information on surviving a downsizing, please reread Chapter 7.)

When you think you have a good understanding of how you can make change work for you, you're ready for A.C.T.

A.C.T.

We may not know exactly what the change will involve, but we know there is more change ahead for us.

Change is a universal human experience. Everyone goes through it. And change in the workplace will continue. We may not know exactly what the change will involve, but we know there is more change ahead for us. We can fight it. Or we can make it work for us.

As Ken Blanchard stated,

■ "If you learn to accept change, communicate about it, and tackle your goals, you can find that change will be a wonderful opportunity to fulfill your dreams and your ambitions."

That's the A.C.T. strategy.

A.C.T. reminds us to:

A: Accept change.

B: Communicate to others.

C: Tackle your goals.

◆ First you accept change. You don't need to like it—you can even grumble about it—but you must accept that change is part of life, and that you, your job, and your employer will continue to go through change. You also should accept that change usually brings new opportunities, that it is continuing, and that you will experience more change by the end of this decade.

◆ Second you communicate with others. It's important to get your reactions out, to vent your anger or frustration when it occurs. It also is important to talk with others about the possibilities that change brings. Communicate with others about the new ideas, the new visions, and the new hopes and goals for the future. People going through change need to communicate!

◆ Third you tackle your new goals and new responsibilities. It's not enough to just talk about them. Talk must give way to action, to doing. The final part of the A.C.T. principle is to tackle the new tasks and to make things work. A.C.T. Act.

Your Plan for Action

Ready? Here is a five-step process to follow as you develop your plan-for-action and resolve to implement it.

1. Assess where you are right now. Briefly describe the organizational change you're going through and how your work unit is reacting to it.

2. Describe your own usual style of reacting to change and how you are reacting to this specific organizational change.

3. Review the list of strategies described in Chapter 3. Select at least three and up to five strategies that you can use to help make change work for you.

4. Review the strategies described in Chapter 5. Select at least three and up to five strategies to help you more effectively manage the stress of an organizational change.

5. Set your plan for action using the following format. Identify the specific strategies you will implement and when you will implement each one.

8

I _____ have read and completed the exercises in **Making Change Work for You!** I will start to implement the following strategies by:

Strategies	Date
_____	_____
_____	_____
_____	_____
_____	_____
_____	_____
_____	_____
_____	_____

Signed _____

You may want to photocopy this action plan out and hang it someplace where you can refer to it. Good Luck!